A library has many **reference books**. Some might be:

Encyclopedia of Wildlife   **Encyclopedia of Sports**   **Thesaurus**
Various Bibliographies   **Unusual Place Names**   **Nature Atlas**
Twentieth Century Writers   **Science Dictionary**   **Music Dictionary**
Encyclopedia of Horses   **Omnibus of Poetry**   **Rhyming Dictionary**

Use these titles to answer the questions.

Which reference book might . . .

1. tell what a harp is? _____

2. have poems by Langston Hughes? _____

3. tell about a town called Wapwallopin? _____

4. show a map of migrating geese? _____

5. tell about the writer of your favorite book? _____

6. have information on racehorses? _____

7. contain bibliographies (lists of books)? _____

8. have information on skiing? _____

9. help you find a word that rhymes with "breeze"? _____

10. tell about rabbits, foxes, and badgers? _____

11. tell about biology and chemistry? _____

12. be a book of words that is not a dictionary? _____

Brainwork! Use the first letter of each answer you wrote to help Paul answer Jeff's

question. _____

1   S0-DVG-401

Karen's dictionary had a Table of Contents. She found many things listed in the dictionary besides spelling and word meanings.

Karen looked at the **Tables of Measurement.** Now she could find how many ounces were in a pound, or how many feet in a mile. The **Metric Conversion Tables** told how to change miles to kilometers and pounds to kilograms. **Morse Code** told how to send messages in dot-dash. **Proofreaders' Symbols** helped Karen understand the marks her teacher put on her writing papers. Karen liked the Codes and Ciphers section best.

Here is a part of the Codes and Ciphers section.

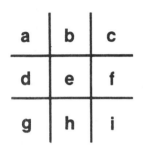 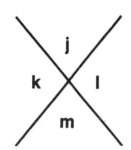 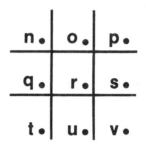 

CODE KEY
Use the code above to decipher this message.

(cipher message, with answer blanks below each word)

___ ___ ___   ___ ___ ___   ___ ___ ___   ___ ___ ___

___ ___ ___ ___   ___ ___   ___   ___ ___ ___ ___ ___ ___ ___ ___

___ ___ ___ ___   ___ ___ ___ ___   ___ ___ ___ ___ ___ ___ ___

___ ___ ___   ___ ___ ___ ___ ___ ___ ___ ___

Brainwork! Find a dictionary that has tables, codes and other information. List the titles of these information sections.

 FS-32018 Fourth Grade Activities

Signs and Symbols
-Astronomy

New Moon
First Quarter Moon
Full Moon
Earth
Sun

Music Symbols

♯ Sharp
♭ Flat
♮ Natural
o Whole Note

Index of First Names and Their Meanings

Alex, Alexander: leader of men

Alice, Allison: of noble rank

Bob, Bobby, Rob, Robert: glory and bright

Carol, Caroline, Carolyn: feminine of
                                                    Charles

Charles: man, warrior

David: beloved

Flora: flower

George: farmer

Harriet, Harriette: fem. of Harry

Harry, Henry: home and kingdom

Susan's father's dictionary had a special section at the back that showed signs, symbols, and names. Some of the information Susan found is shown above. Use it to answer the questions.

1. Draw the symbol for the sun. _____

2. Write the meaning of David. _____

3. Show two symbols for the Full Moon. _____

4. Draw the symbol for a musical sharp. _____

5. What does Flora mean? _____

6. Draw three symbols for the earth. _____

7. Draw one symbol for the first quarter of the moon. _____

8. What names mean the same as Robert? _____

9. What does Harriette mean? (Hint: see what Harry means.) _____

_____

Brainwork! Look in a large dictionary to see what your name means. _____

_____ . If your name is on this page,

find out what the symbol © means. _____

Henry's Horse
by
William Freitag
illustrated by
Dorothy Shepherd

Published by
Maris Gibson Co.
Dallas, Pennsylvania

Copyright 1981
William Freitag

All rights reserved.

CONTENTS

Find and write in the correct answers.

The title page of Danny's library book tells us

1. the title of the book _____

2. who wrote it (the author) _____

3. who drew the pictures (the illustrator) _____

4. what company published the book _____

5. the city where it was published _____

The back of the title page tells us the date when the book was copyrighted:

_____

Danny noticed all his textbooks had a title page with the author's name, sometimes an illustrator, and the publisher's name and city. Some of the books had more than one author.

Brainwork! Look at the title pages of some of your textbooks. Write the titles, authors, publishers, city, and copyright dates on the chart below.

Subject	Title	Author(s)	Publisher	City	Date
Math					
Spelling					
Social Studies					
Science					

At the back of Kerry's atlas is a section called a **gazetteer**. A **gazetteer** is a geographical dictionary that lists all the places and geographical features in an atlas. Cities, states, rivers, and towns are listed alphabetically. A number in parentheses () after city, state, and county names gives the population. In **boldface** type after the page numbers are letters and numbers. These are called map coordinates. They help to locate a place on the map.

Here is a section of Kerry's **gazetteer**.

Columbia, Missouri (36,655) ....page 56	**D 8**	
Columbia, South Carolina (260,830) ....page 71	**G 5**	
Columbia Dam (Alabama) ....page 34	**B 2**	
Columbia Lake (British Columbia) .....page 91	**A 7**	
Columbia Mountains (Mexico) ....page 99	**M 4**	
Columbia River (U.S. and Canada) ....page 92	**F 8**	
Columbia Falls, Maine (442) ....page 43	**A 1**	

The map of Columbia, South Carolina, is on page _____. Its population is

_____ . Columbia Lake is in _____ _____ . It is shown on the map on

page _____ . Its coordinates are ___ ___ . The Columbia _____ is in the U.S.

and Canada. Columbia Falls, Maine, has a population of _____ . The

coordinates for Columbia dam are ___ ___ . Which city named Columbia has the

largest population? _____ .

Brainwork! Find your town or city in the **gazetteer** of an atlas. Write its population

_____ ,the page _____ , and coordinates _____ .

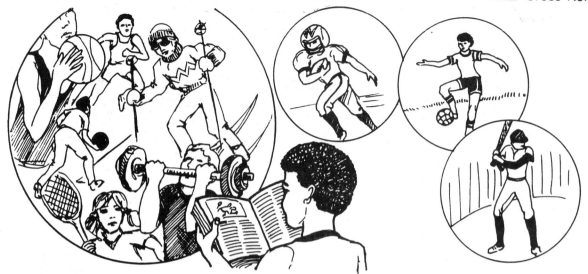

George could not find the information he needed under <u>Sports</u> in his encyclopedia. At the end of the Sports article it said, "See also Baseball, Football, Soccer." George looked under the **cross reference**, Football, and found what he needed to know.

Use an encyclopedia to find what cross references are listed under the subjects below. If there are none, write "none." Write the name of the encyclopedia you

used here. _____

1. Rattlesnakes _____

2. Hoover Dam _____

3. Mistletoe _____

4. Sahara _____

5. Henry VIII of England _____

6. Bogotá _____

7. Clarinet _____

8. Laser _____

9. Spiders _____

10. Broccoli _____

Brainwork! Look in the encyclopedia for <u>Michelangelo</u>. Write two paragraphs about this topic on the back of this paper.

Kimi found a shelf of special encyclopedias in the library. Each of these books was about only one general subject: music, birds, painting, others.

Write the name of the special subject encyclopedia to use on the line after each statement.

1. Mel's hobby is unusual wild animals. _____

2. Anne plays the clarinet. _____

3. Jamie wants to raise orchids. _____

4. Rob needs facts on soccer. _____

5. Melissa is a bird watcher. _____

6. Chris must report on a composer. _____

7. Bill wants to know about eagles. _____

8. Laurie is collecting coins. _____

9. Sue wants to know about tennis. _____

10. Mike is interested in oil paintings. _____

Brainwork! Make up a title for a special encyclopedia that would help you learn more about your own hobby, favorite sport, or other interest.

_____

Jody's library has two card catalogs. One is labeled **Title/Author**. If Jody knows the title or author of a book she wants, she looks in that catalog. Jody looked at these cards.

Author Card →

751.422 Galvin, Ellen

Gal   Watercolor pa

Maris Gibson

115 p.

Title Card

751.422   Watercolor Painting

Gal

Galvin, Ellen

Watercolor painting.

Maris Gibson Co, Dallas, Pa, 1981.

115 p.   illus.   photos   plates

Jody wants to find the books below. If she should look for a title card, write title. If she should look for an author card, write author.

1. Little American _____

2. James Scott _____

3. My Friend Joe _____

4. Johnny Onenote _____

5. Paul Simpson _____

6. Another Day _____

7. Mary Bleck _____

8. John L. Smith _____

9. Your Horoscope _____

10. Memories of Yesterday _____

11. James M. Bradley _____

12. Raising Orchids _____

Underline the last name of each author above. Author cards are filed alphabetically according to last name.

Brainwork! What is the call number of the library book you are reading? ____

_____ . If you do not have a library book,

look for one in the library and write its call number.

8   FS-32018 Fourth Grade Activities

Kevin wanted to learn how to do watercolor painting. He looked in the library's **subject catalog** under Watercolor Painting. A card said, "See PAINTING." Kevin chose this card:

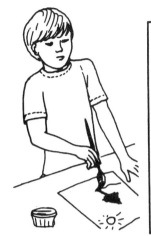

> 751.422 PAINTING
> Gal Galvin, Ellen
> Watercolor painting.
> Maris Gibson Co., Dallas, PA, 1981.
> 115 p.   illus.   photos   plates
>   Illustrated step-by-step lessons in
>   beginning watercolor technique.
>
> 1. Painting   I. Author   II. Title

1. What is the call number of this book? _____

2. Who wrote the book? _____

3. What is its title? _____

4. Who published the book? _____

5. In what city was the book published? _____

6. What is the copyright date of the book? _____

7. How is the book illustrated? _____

8. Why do you think it might be a good book for beginners who want to

learn about watercolor painting? _____

9. Why would the book be less useful if it had no illustrations? _____

_____

10. What is the subject under which the book is filed? _____

Brainwork! Find three library books about Watercolor Painting. Write the titles.

_____

_____

Libraries put books on their shelves according to a special system. Most libraries use the **Dewey Decimal System**. In the Dewey Decimal System, books are put into categories or groups.

Books numbered: are about:

000-099	general reference, encyclopedias
100-199	philosophy, thoughts, ideas
200-299	religion, myths
300-399	social science, folklore, fairy tales
400-499	languages, dictionaries
500-599	pure science: math, astronomy, botany, zoology, physics, chemistry, earth science
600-699	technology (useful sciences): medicine, engineering, home economics, agriculture
700-799	fine arts: music, art, drawing, sports, hobbies, photography
800-899	literature, plays, poetry
900-999	history, geography, travel

Write the Dewey Decimal category (Example: 500-599) after the titles below to show where these books would be shelved.

Grimm's Fairy Tales _____   **Dictionary of Language** _____

History of Europe _____   **Travel in Japan** _____

Photography _____   **Music for Strings** _____

Greek Myths _____   **Poetry, a Collection** _____

Philosophy of Mankind _____   **Medicine and Surgery** _____

Brainwork! Browse through the library shelves. Write the names of three books that have the call numbers between 600 and 699.

_____

Unscramble the words to find out what Simon says.

Jason: Where should I look first for information for my science project?

Simon: Your <u>niceecs</u> book. _____

Pam: I need to know. Where should I start?

Simon: Try your <u>nauggeal</u> book. _____

Molly: Where can I find facts about the United States?

Simon: Your <u>ilacssotiedus</u> book, of course. _____

When you need to know something about one of your school subjects such as math, science, social studies, language, or spelling, a good place to look first is in your textbook.

Write the kinds of textbooks you would use to find the following information.

1. measurement tables _____

2. punctuation _____

3. geographical terms _____

4. the order of the Solar System _____

5. rules for spelling the long e sound _____

6. correct form for a friendly letter _____

7. a list of U.S. presidents _____

8. metric measurement tables _____

9. maps of the world's rainfall _____

10. glossary of scientific terms _____

Brainwork! List three more kinds of information you can find in your math book.

_____

_____

Larry asked the librarian to help him find information for his report on African elephants. She showed Larry magazines which had articles on elephants.

In the column on the left are some magazine names. In the column on the right are some report topics assigned to Mrs. Smith's class. Match the magazines with the topics. Write the numbers of the magazines you should use on the line after the topics. You may use each title more than once.

1. **Animal Life** (1)

2. **Miniature Models** (2)

3. **Geographical Survey** (3)

4. **African Report** (4)

5. **Space and Stars** (5)

6. **Science Monthly** (6)

7. **Art Then and Now** (7)

8. **Railroad Miniatures** (8)

9. **Dollhouse Annual** (9)

10. **Solar Magazine** (10)

11. **News of the Week** (11)

12. **History Monthly** (12)

artists of yesterday and today _____

space shuttle _____

doll house miniatures _____

wild animals of Africa _____

model railroads _____

the events of this week _____

life in the Arctic _____

black hole in space _____

the national elections _____

100 years ago in America _____

American Indian art _____

African art _____

Brainwork! Which of the magazines above might have information on Satellites?

_____ Last week's election? _____ Wolverines? _____

Name _____ Date _____

Tom read several articles in different magazines to get information for his report. His teacher asked him to list the articles he read at the end of his report. Tom wrote his Bibliography like this:

1) Author's last name, then first name. 2) title of the article. 3) name of magazine (underlined), 4) date of magazine.

Arrange the information below in the correct order with the correct punctuation.

a) <u>News Monthly</u>, June 1980, "Cattle Foods." Jane Galvin

b) Maria Mitchell, January 1887, "A New Comet." <u>Science Monthly</u>

c) October 1981, <u>Science and Fiction</u>, Brad Berry. "New Start."

d) "Cosmic Cosmos." January 1967, W.C. Are. <u>Scientific Review</u>

e) May 1978, "Atlantis Found." <u>Exploration</u>, Jan Jones

	Author — (last name first)	Title of Article	Name of Magazine (underlined)	Date
Ex.	Jones, Jan. "Atlantis Found." <u>Exploration</u>, May 1978 .			
a.				
b.				
c.				
d.				

Brainwork! Find an article in a magazine that you can use in a report. Write down the author's name, the title of the article, the name of the magazine, and its date.

_____

_____

 FS-32018 Fourth Grade Activities

Name _____ Date _____

Joey always read the page in the newspaper that gave the complete weather report. He studied the weather maps and the pictures taken by satellite.

Here are some reports of the weather in several cities.

City	Lo/Hi	Precipitation	City	Lo/Hi	Precipitation
Albany	33/56	----	Juneau	43/49	1.61
Atlanta	59/83	----	Miami Beach	70/79	----
Boise	36/68	----	New York	44/66	----
Chicago	43/63	.17	Reno	26/70	----
Dallas	71/87	.03	St. Louis	62/69	1.10
Flagstaff	28/55	----	Spokane	31/61	----

1. Which city had the lowest low temperature? _____

2. Where was the hottest high? _____

3. Where did it rain or snow (precip.)? _____

_____

4. Which city had the most rain or snow? _____

5. Which cities had below-freezing (32°) lows? _____

_____

6. Which city had the greatest difference between low and high? _____

By how many degrees? _____

7. Which city had the least difference between high and low? _____

By how many degrees? _____

Brainwork! Find the complete weather report in your paper. What city had the highest high? _____ The lowest low? _____

14   FS-32018 Fourth Grade Activities

The **classified** section of Terry's phone book (Yellow Pages) comes after the white pages. In some cities this is a separate book. Yellow Pages have advertisements as well as alphabetical listings within each **classification**. Some **classifications** are:

Automobile Body Repair
Automobile Dealers — New Cars
Automobile Dealers — Used Cars
Dog & Cat Doctors — See Veterinarians
Dog and Cat Grooming
Dolls
Florists — Retail
Florists — Wholesale
Hobby and Model Supplies
Judo, Karate, and Jujitsu
Kindergartens — See Nursery Schools
Moccasins — See Shoes, Retail

Modeling Schools
Motorcycles
Music Dealers — See
   Musical Instruments, Records,
   Phonograph, Stereophonic Equipment
Nurseries — Plants & Trees
Nursery Schools
Pizzas
Public Schools — See Schools,
   Elementary & Secondary
Skate Boards

If you want to call about . . .   **look under . . .**

1. a sick dog _____

2. model airplane kits _____

3. ordering a pizza _____

4. renting a clarinet _____

5. buying a rosebush _____

6. reporting sick at school _____

7. ordering flowers for Mom _____

8. kindergartens for sister Sue _____

9. repairing a dented fender _____

10. a bath and brushing for Fido _____

11. karate lessons _____

12. a pair of moccasins _____

Brainwork! Write the difference between **retail** and **wholesale**.

Mr. Quinn's **almanac** has almost 1000 pages of facts and information. Andrea found a table of distances like this:

	Albuquerque	Chicago	Denver	Los Angeles	New Orleans	Seattle
Albuquerque	----	1285	482	805	1145	1511
Chicago	1285	----	1018	2106	929	2013
Denver	482	1018	----	1162	1284	1377
Los Angeles	805	2106	1162	----	1916	1177
New Orleans	1145	929	1284	1916	----	2645
Seattle	1511	2013	1377	1177	2645	----

To find the distance from Los Angeles to Denver, find Los Angeles on the left side and Denver at the top. Run your finger across from Los Angeles and down from Denver. Where they meet you will find the distance, 1162 miles.

1. How far is it from Chicago to Seattle? _____

2. What is the distance from Los Angeles to Chicago? _____

3. How many miles from Albuquerque to New Orleans? _____

4. Which two cities are closest together? _____

5. Which two cities are farthest apart? _____

6. Which is farther, Denver to New Orleans or Chicago to Albuquerque? ____

_____

7. Is Denver closer to Albuquerque or New Orleans? _____

8. Is Seattle closer to Denver or Los Angeles? _____

Brainwork! Find a table of distances in an almanac or other reference book. Find the distance from your city, or the nearest city to your home, to New

York. _____ To San Francisco _____

To Miami _____

Bibliography

Adams, Henry. <u>Blue Whale</u>. New York: Couzzins Publishing Co., 1980.

Capper, Janet. <u>Dolphins</u>. Cincinnati: Scientific Publishers and
    Textbook Company, 1981.

Smith, John and **Matthew** Vassar. <u>Grey Whales</u>. Dallas: Times Co., 1979.

Wells, Marta. <u>Sea Mammals</u>. Chicago: Illustrated Press, 1981.

This is the example Mrs. Collins gave her class to show them how to make a **Bibliography**. She told the class they must put a Bibliography of the books they had used at the end of their reports. She gave them these rules:

1) For each book, list the author's last name, then first name.
2) Next list the title. Underline it.
3) Next list the city where the book was published, the publisher and date.
4) Put in commas, periods, and colons as shown above.
5) List all the books alphabetically according to the author's last name.
6) If an entry takes more than one line, indent all following lines.

Use scratch paper to list these books correctly. Then arrange them in correct alphabetical order on the lines below.

1. Stuart Publishing   1981   Chicago   by   M.L. Smith   Reptiles

2. by Alex Apple   Boston   Crown Co.   Frogs   1976

3. Denver   Post and Sons   1982   Amphibians   by Jim Misch

4. 1979   Toads and Frogs   May Co.   by Bill Rawson   Miami

_____

_____

_____

_____

Brainwork! Use a book in your desk to make a correct bibliography entry.

Mrs. Pollack's class uses this chart of **proofreading symbols**.

Symbol	Meaning
∧	add the word above the **caret** (∧)
l.c.	use lower case (small letters)
cap.	use capital letter
w.w.	wrong word - see correct word in margin
sp.	spelling error - look it up
p.	punctuation error circled - see correction above
¶	make a new paragraph; indent it
frag	fragment, not a complete sentence
RO	run-on sentence, break up into two or more
M	keep a straight margin
→	indent the beginning of a paragraph 1 inch

Rewrite the paragraph below correctly. Use the chart to find out what the marks mean. There are 12 errors.

```
  →        l.c.              RO
   My new Bike is a racer  it is red and silver.
        to            frag.           sp.
M  I like∧ride it downhill. Sometimes up. It gose
                ¶  w.w.
When   so fast it's like flying. Then I ride to school,
            sp.              cap.       p.
       all my freinds want to try it. I let john ride ○
```

_____

_____

_____

_____

_____

_____

Brainwork! Trade papers with a friend and proofread each other's work.

When Muffy writes a report, she has difficulty telling all about her topic. Mrs. Chilton thinks this is because Muffy chooses topics that are too **general**. She tells Muffy to choose just one part of a topic. When Muffy writes about her state, Iowa, Mrs. Chilton suggests that Muffy **narrow down** the topic to "Iowa's Products" or "Important Events in Iowa."

Match the **narrowed-down** topic below to the **general** topic. Write the number of the narrow topic on the line beside the general one.

1. Trees that Lose Their Leaves	Abraham Lincoln _____
2. My Brother's Dune Buggy	The Pilgrims _____
3. How I Spent My Allowance	Christmas _____
4. The First Thanksgiving	Astronomy _____
5. Making Chocolate Chip Cookies	Living Things _____
6. The Battle of Gettysburg	Football _____
7. Young Abraham Lincoln	Cars _____
8. Our Game Last Saturday	The American Revolution _____
9. Five Important Rivers	The Civil War _____
10. Minerals Found In Our County	Mountains _____
11. The Flight of the Space Shuttle	Minerals _____
12. Washington at Valley Forge	Space _____
13. Interesting Christmas Customs	Cooking _____
14. Comets	Rivers _____
15. Mount McKinley	Money _____

Brainwork! Write a narrowed-down topic to use instead of the general topic
American Presidents. _____

You have to write a report on Hawaii. Your Social Studies textbook has these entries in the Index under Hawaii:

climate, 236   history, 237   people, 238
facts, 242   location, 235   photos, 241
government, 239   map, 236   weather, 236

The encyclopedia article is 25 pages long. You would rather not read all of it. You look at the headings in **boldface** type. They are:

Facts About Hawaii   **Food**   **Places to Visit**
Government   **Climate**   **Products**
Politics   **Clothing**   **History**
People   **Education**   **Language**

The library has a shelf of books on Hawaii. Some are:

Hawaii in Pictures   Orchids of Hawaii   Hawaiian Birds

Hawaii, a History   Early Hawaii   Hawaiian Volcanoes

You decide to write about Hawaii's history.

Underline all the index references, encyclopedia headings, and books you would be sure to read to learn about the history of Hawaii.

Put a B beside the topics you would read for general background information.

Brainwork! Use your textbook, or one you borrow from the school, and a library book, plus an encyclopedia. Read the references on Hawaii's history. Take notes. Write a short report on Hawaii's history. Use your own words!

Box Art

Choose only one of the following—crayons, felt tip markers, colored pencils, or water colors.
Then color the designs according to the steps below.

☐ Color box 1 using all different colors.

☐ Select one color. Color box 2 using black, white and different shades (light to dark) of the selected color.

☐ Color box 3 using only warm colors (yellows, oranges, and reds). Color box 4 using only cool colors (greens, blues, and purples).

☐ Vincent Van Gogh was an artist who used long strokes or lines in much of his work. Color box 5 like box 1, but use lines instead of solid coloring to fill the spaces.

☐ Georges Seurat was an artist who used small dots and brush strokes to make the shapes and colors blend. Color box 6 like box 1, but use only dots to draw the design.

Name _____

Directions:

☐ Write the letter above the soccer ball in box 1 below.

☐ Write the letter on the baseball in box 3.

☐ Write the letter on the soccer ball in box 6.

☐ Write the letter to the left of the baseball in box 8.

☐ Write the letter to the right of the football in box 4.

☐ Write the letter to the right of the soccer ball in box 10.

☐ Write the letter on the hockey stick in box 2.

☐ Write the letter above the football in box 5.

☐ Write the letter on the left side of the hockey stick in box 7.

☐ Write the letter on the football on box 9.

above ↑
left ← → right
below ↓

1	2	3	4
T			

5	6	7	8	9	10

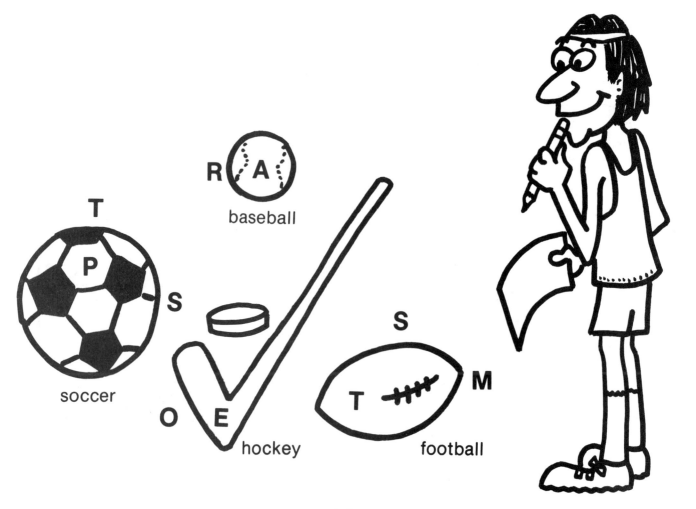

baseball

soccer

hockey

football

Name ______________________________

Directions: The ★ team and • team are playing baseball. The ★ team is up to bat.

- ☐ Make ten ★s in the Star Dugout.
- ☐ Make five •s in the Circle Dugout.
- ☐ Put a • next to [1], [2] and [3].
- ☐ On the scoreboard write 2 for • and 3 for ★.
- ☐ Draw a line to show the path of the ball from
  pitcher• to ★ at [H]
  [H] ★ to right field •
  right field• back to pitcher•.
- ☐ Draw a dotted line----- to show path of ★ hitter from
  [H] to [1]
  [1] to [2]
  [2] to [3]

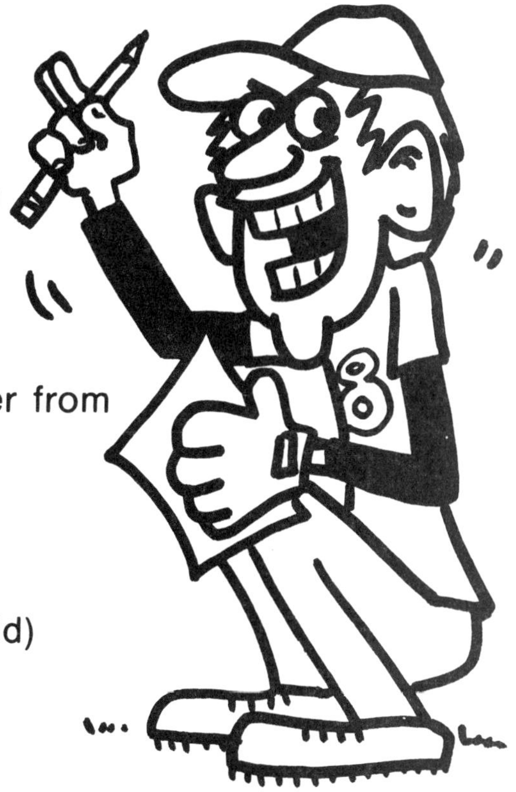

(center field)
•

Scoreboard	
•	★

(left field)
•

(right field)
•

Star Dugout

[2]

(short stop)
•

(pitcher)

[3] • [1]

[H] ★ (hitter)
•
(catcher)

Circle Dugout

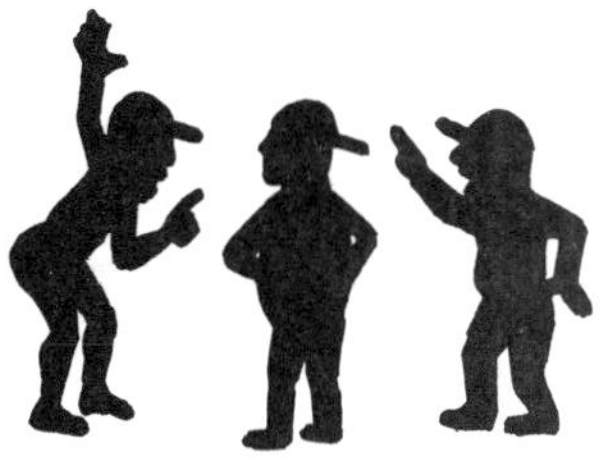

Name _____

Directions: Mark each statement true or false by coloring the ○ . Then write the underlined letter in the blanks below. The number in ( ) tells you where to write the letter.

	True	False
☑ Dogs can laugh. (5)	○	●
☐ You can pick up a puppy. (3)	○	○
☐ You can't pick up an elephant. (12)	○	○
☐ Girls can be truck drivers. (6)	○	○
☐ All food must be cooked before eaten. (4)	○	○
☐ A feather is lighter than a book. (7)	○	○
☐ Children are younger than adults. (11)	○	○
☐ Hamburger is a vegetable. (1)	○	○
☐ A turtle's shell protects its soft body. (9)	○	○
☐ Apples are a kind of fruit. (8)	○	○
☐ Hot water can burn you. (2)	○	○
☐ Ice cubes are cold. (10)	○	○
☐ Young dogs are called kittens. (13)	○	○

To follow directions you must:

___ ___ ___ ___ C ___ ___ ___ ___ ___ ___ ___ ___ .
 1   2   3   4 5 6   7   8   9 10 11 12 13

Name _____

You will get better grades if you

___ ___ ___ ___ ___ ___ ___ ___ ___ ___ ___ on the directions!
 1   2   3   4   5   6   7   8   9   10 11

Directions: Write letters on the lines above to find the missing word. Write the underlined letter on:

line #1 of the word that comes first in the dictionary.
c̲ube   cu̲p   cudd̲le

line #5 of the word that does not belong.
appl̲e   ban̲ana   be̲d

line #3 of the word that names the highest number.
tw̲o   ten̲   t̲hree

line #11 of the word that names the lowest number.
fifte̲en   twenty̲   f̲ifty

line #9 of the word that names the tallest animal.
lion̲   gira̲ffe   m̲onkey

line #4 of the word that names the heaviest thing.
feath̲er   bo̲ok   c̲ar

line #7 of the thing that will float.
t̲oothpick   roc̲k   pin̲

line #6 of the thing that will not float.
n̲ail   toothpic̲k   b̲oat

line #8 of the word that names the smallest animal.
d̲og   cat̲   r̲at

line #2 of the animal that makes no sound.
cat̲   d̲og   g̲oldfish

line #10 of the thing that is not alive.
tre̲e   t̲ruck   bir̲d

25   FS-32018 Fourth Grade Activities

Directions: In the soccer game between △ team and ○ team, 🔺11 has the ball (●). Draw a dotted line to show the path of the ball. Check each one off as you finish it.

☐ 🔺11 passes to 🔺5 .

☐ 🔺5 passes ball to 🔺4 .

☐ 🔺4 tries to make a goal but it is stopped by ⑤ .

☐ ⑤ kicks the ball out to ① .

☐ ① passes it to ⑧ .

☐ ⑧ kicks the ball into the goal behind 🔺1 .

☐ Write 1 on the scoreboard for ○ team. They need two more goals to have the same score as △ team.

☐ Write the score on the scoreboard for △ team.

Scoreboard	
△	○

Bits and Pieces

Use a ruler to divide the square into equal "bits and pieces" by following these steps.

☐ Use one vertical (|) line and one horizontal (_) line to divide this square into fourths (four equal parts).

☐ Using only two lines, divide the top left square into fourths.

☐ Using only two lines, find another way to divide the bottom right square into fourths.

☐ Using three lines, divide the top right square into fourths.

☐ Using three lines, find another way to divide the bottom left square into fourths.

The original square is now made up of 16 pieces. Even though they are different shapes, each piece is equal in area and is 1/16 of the square.

☐ Color the triangles green. The triangles equal 4/16 or 1/4 of the entire square.

☐ Color the squares red. The squares equal 4/16 or 1/4 of the entire square.

☐ Color the rectangles blue. The rectangles equal 8/16 or 2/4 or 1/2 of the entire square.

Brainwork! Write directions for dividing a rectangle into eighths.

MONEY FACT$

Read each statement carefully. If the first part of the statement is true, do what it says. If it is false, go on to the next problem. Begin with $10.00. Add to or subtract from the money as you go along. The first one has been done for you.

☑ If George Washington appears on a $1.00 bill, give yourself a dollar.	$ 10.00
	+ $ 1.00
☐ If a nickel is worth half a dime, give yourself two nickels.	$ 11.00
☐ If two bucks equals two dollars, subtract two bucks from your subtotal. (A "buck" is slang for a dollar.)	$
☐ If Abraham Lincoln appears on both a $5.00 bill and a penny, subtract $5.01 from your current subtotal.	$
	$
☐ If 40 quarters = $10.00, give yourself $10.00.	$
☐ If five grand equals five thousand dollars, give yourself five grand. (A "grand" is slang for a $1,000.)	$
	$
☐ If Thomas Jefferson appears on a nickel, subtract nine nickels from your current subtotal.	$
	$
☐ If two quarters, three dimes and one nickel are worth more than six dimes and six nickels, give yourself five quarters.	$
	$
☐ If you can use nickels, dimes, and quarters to get seven coins to equal one dollar, give yourself $1.00. Write the combination of coins here.	$
	$
	$
	$
☐ If your grand total equals $5,014.64, pat yourself on the back.	$
	$

penny   nickel

dime

quarter

Brainwork! Write two directions to get your grand total to $6,000.

FS-32018 Fourth Grade Activities

Directions: Put the answers on the Magic Math Square.

Z	E	J	S
D	**Y**	**M** 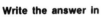	**T**
W	**C**	**R**	**Q**
V	**K**	**I**	**G**

Write the answer in

☐ 12 − 8 + 1 = 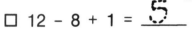 M

☐ 2 × _____ = 20 I

☐ 4 + 2 + 7 = _____ E

☐ 8 − 6 + _____ = 6 Q

☐ _____ × 9 = 18 K

☐ 100 − 99 = _____ G

☐ 20 − _____ = 15 Z

☐ 2 × 5 + 1 = _____ C

☐ 11 − 3 − 2 = _____ J

☐ 100 − 98 = _____ D

☐ 11 − 11 + 5 = _____ R

☐ 10 + 4 + 5 = _____ T

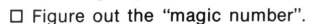

Magic Math Squares add up to the same total in each row going across→ or down↓.

☐ Figure out the "magic number".

☐ The "magic number" is ___ ___ .

☐ Fill in the **answers** to the four empty squares.

35

Name _____

Directions: To find out the name of the state for each bird, write the letters on the
   correct lines as follows:

☐ Write the middle three letters of <u>stone</u> on lines 30, 31 and 32.
☐ On lines 4, 5, and 6 write the first three letters of <u>riddle</u>.
☐ On lines 24, 25 and 26 write the last three letters of <u>lash</u>.
☐ On line 17 write the middle letter in <u>nap</u>.
☐ Write the three middle letters in <u>paint</u> on lines 19, 20 and 21.
☐ On lines 11 and 12 write the middle two letters of <u>lift</u>.
☐ Write the first letter in <u>eye</u> on line 22.
☐ On lines 13, 14 and 15 write the last three letters of <u>corn</u>.
☐ On line 18 write the first letter of <u>mother</u>.
☐ On line 23 write the last letter of <u>cow</u>.
☐ Write the middle three letters of <u>scalp</u> on lines 8, 9 and 10.
☐ On lines 27, 28 and 29 write the last three letters of <u>talking</u>.
☐ On line 7 write the middle letter of <u>rag</u>.
☐ Write the first letter of <u>inside</u> on line 16.
☐ On lines 1, 2 and 3 write the three beginning letters of <u>float</u>.
☐ Capitalize the first letter of each state.

State Birds

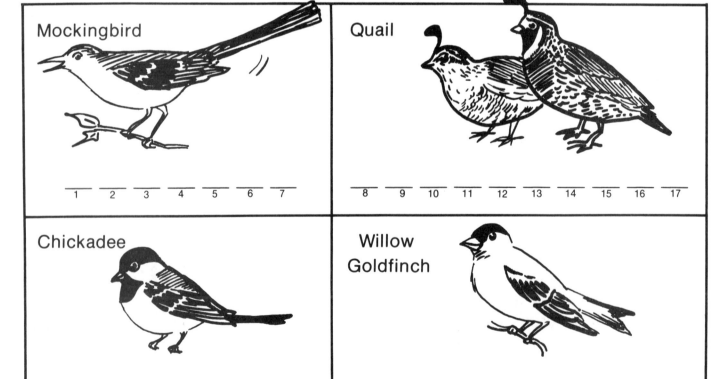

A Wall of Words

Follow the directions on each brick. Start with brick **1** and move in numerical order.

1. Use the letters in your first and last names to make four words.

2. In brick **3** design a word that looks like its meaning. Example:

3.
SHAKY

4. Skip the next brick.

5. Write a ten letter word that begins with a vowel.

6. A palindrome is a word that reads the same backward as it does forward. Write a palindrome on brick **7**.
Example: dad

7.

8. Write ten two-letter words.

9. An antonym is a word that means the opposite of a given word. Write five antonyms for *ugly*.

10. An onomatopoeic word sounds like the noise it represents (tick tock, buzz). Write two onomatopoeic words on the next brick.

11.

12. Write a five-syllable word. Draw a slash between each syllable. Example: hip/po/pot/a/mus

13. Decode and write the following message: **Cn y rd ths mssg?**

14.

Using the same code, write **The End** on brick **14**.

Brainwork! Design a new brick for the "Wall of Words" puzzle.

Bright Balloons

A synonym is a word that means the same or about the same as another word. *Frightened* is a synonym for *scared*. Read and follow the directions below carefully. If you are not sure what a word means, look it up in a dictionary.

- ☐ Color the balloons yellow that contain a synonym for *tired*.
- ☐ Color the balloons orange that contain a synonym for *loud*.
- ☐ Color the balloons red that contain a synonym for *pretty*.
- ☐ Color the balloons purple that contain a synonym for *look*.
- ☐ Color the balloons blue that contain a synonym for *talk*.

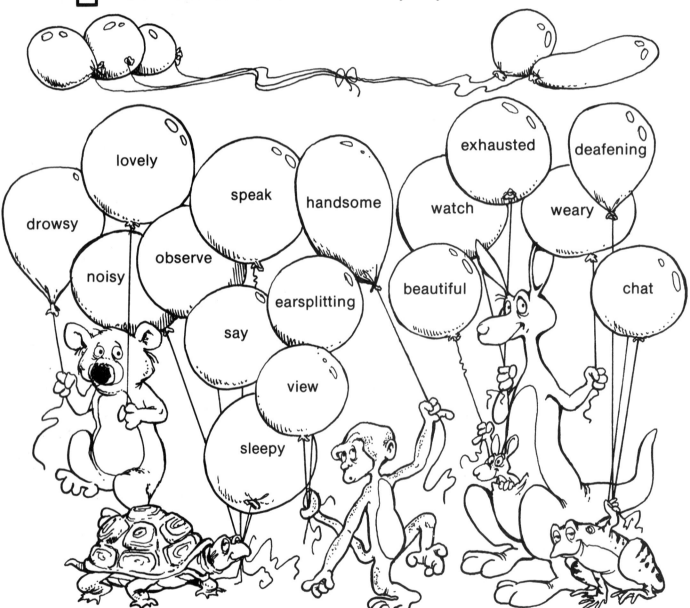

Brainwork! Draw a balloon. Inside the balloon, write another synonym for one of the words above. Then color it correctly.

38

Name _____

Directions:

☐ Circle the words that should be capitalized.

Kim and mary went to jane's house.

☐ Draw a dotted line under two animals.

dog   spoon   fork   frog   apple

☐ Put an **X** on things that are not alive.

tree   whale   pen   rain   letter

☐ Circle three things that float.

rock   penny   boat   toothpick   twig

☐ Draw a box around two things to eat.

box   bread   fork   meat   string

☐ Draw a line through things not made of metal.

toothpick   car   string   paste   scissors

☐ Underline things found inside a house.

rug   tub   beds   grass   gate   table

☐ Draw a line to make two words (base/ball).

mailman   classroom   blackboard   underground

☐ Underline the words. Circle the endings (-s -ed -ing).

looked   talking   rains   sooner   hats   seeing

☐ Mark the long vowel. Cross out the silent vowel (kitͤ).

gate   cute   kite   hide   rise   wide   late

☐ Put an **X** on words that are spelled wrong.

Her babby won't stip criing.

☐ Circle short vowel words. Put a box around long vowel words.

hat   glide   slip   wipe   kite   ran   his

 FS-32018 Fourth Grade Activities

Name _____

Directions:

☐ Count across→, then up↑ on the grid to make words.

☐ Write the words on the **word list**.

☐ Find the meaning for each word.

☐ Write the number of the word in the ◯ by its meaning.

Word List →↑

① C O A T
   4,3 5,5 1,3 5,4

② ___ ___ ___ ___ ___
   3,4 5,2 1,3 1,5 2,1

③ ___ ___ ___ ___ ___
   3,4 5,4 5,5 4,1 2,1

④ ___ ___ ___ ___
   5,4 5,5 1,5 4,1

⑤ ___ ___ ___ ___ ___
   4,3 1,5 1,3 5,4 2,1

⑥ ___ ___ ___ ___
   5,2 2,1 1,3 1,5

⑦ ___ ___ ___ ___ ___
   4,3 5,5 1,3 3,4 5,4

⑧ ___ ___ ___ ___ ___
   3,4 3,5 1,3 1,5 5,4

⑨ ___ ___ ___ ___
   5,4 1,5 1,3 5,2

⑩ ___ ___ ___ ___
   1,5 2,1 1,3 1,5

Grid

6						
5	R		M		O	
4			S		T	
3	A			C		
2					P	
1		E		N		
Start	1	2	3	4	5	6

Word Meanings

◯ ripped   ◯ extra

◯ rock   ◯ jacket

◯ back   ◯ bright

◯ fruit   ◯ catch

◯ roll along   ◯ box

Name _____

Directions: Which underlined word comes first in abc order? Make an X or O in the correct place on the Tic Tac Toe grid. Check the ☐ as you follow each direction.

☐ Make X in ☐ if <u>airport</u> comes before <u>alike</u>.
☐ Make O in ☐ if <u>barn</u> comes before <u>base</u>.
☐ Make X in ☐ if <u>dog</u> comes before <u>dust</u>.
☐ Make O in ☐ if <u>today</u> comes before <u>tool</u>.
☐ Make X in ☐ if <u>leg</u> comes before <u>left</u>.
☐ Make O in ☐ if <u>week</u> comes before <u>weed</u>.
☐ Make X in ☐ if <u>puppy</u> comes before <u>question</u>.
☐ Make O in ☐ if <u>feather</u> comes before <u>five</u>.
☐ Make X in ☐ if <u>tag</u> comes before <u>talk</u>.
☐ Make O in ☐ if <u>many</u> comes before <u>mark</u>.
☐ Make X in ☐ if <u>noise</u> comes before <u>north</u>.
☐ Who won? X or O ? _____

ⓈPelling Sleuth

Become a spelling sleuth by carefully following the directions on the notebook paper.

CLUE 1

The family had just eaten chocolate cake for desert.

_____ _____

CLUE 2

Suspect was last seen in the sience room.

_____

_____

CLUE 3

Several dimonds are missing from the jewlry store.

_____

_____

CLUE 4

Forteen rats escaped from the lab.

_____ _____

CLUE 5

A child's pair of sissors was found near the suspect's bicicle.

_____

_____

CLUE 6

There party lasted two hours.

_____

CLUE 7

Her cousin is missing, too.

_____ _____

CLUE 8

The suspect was not at scool today.

_____ _____

CLUE 9

Goverment agents are working on this case.

_____

_____

CLUE 10

The date of the crime was Wensday, Febuary 17, 1987.

_____

_____

Directions

☐ Circle the misspelled words in the clues. If you find 12, go to the next step. If not, look again.

☐ If a clue has two misspelled words, write those words correctly on the blank lines.

☐ If a clue has only one misspelled word, write that word correctly on the second blank.

☐ On the back of this sheet, list in alphabetical order the words whose spellings you've corrected. Draw a box around the last word.

☐ To discover the suspect's name, cross out the third, fifth, sixth, and eighth letters of the boxed word. Write the suspect's name here:

Brainwork! Correctly write two other words you have trouble spelling. Use the dictionary to check your spelling.

Name _____

Directions:

☐ Circle the three things in each row that are alike.

☐ Underline the word that does not belong.

☐ Count the vowels in the underlined words and mark the Vowel Count Chart.

☐ Answer the questions below the chart.

1.	plum	peach	apple	potato
2.	shirt	hat	eyes	pants
3.	car	walls	windows	roof
4.	bed	pencil	chair	table
5.	kangaroo	lion	goldfish	tiger
6.	train	bus	plane	ticket
7.	dime	penny	dollar	nickel
8.	kitten	lady	baby	man

Vowel Count Chart: Color one ☐ for each vowel in the eight underlined words.

How many?

a								
e								
i								
o								
u								

Questions: On the Vowel Count Chart which vowel appears:

the most _____

the least _____

the same _____ and _____

Name _____

Directions:
☐ Look for letters that should be capitalized.
☐ Fill in the answer box to show where the capital should be.
☐ Mark <u>no mistakes</u> if there are no missing capitals.

1.
1)	Mary, Jane and
2)	nan are my
3)	friends.
4)	no mistakes

2.
1)	Ted is looking
2)	for John's house
3)	on Maple Street.
4)	no mistakes

3.
1)	In mexico the
2)	weather is
3)	very warm.
4)	no mistakes

4.
1)	Daddy's birthday
2)	is the last
3)	day of july.
4)	no mistakes

Answer Box

1. ① ② ③ ④   3. ① ② ③ ④
2. ① ② ③ ④   4. ① ② ③ ④

Directions:
☐ Look for letters that should be capitalized.
☐ Fill in the ◯ under the part of the sentence that needs a capital.
☐ Mark none if no capitals are needed.

1. We met Mary	in New york	last summer.	None
◯	◯	◯	◯

2. Every August	i go to camp	in Texas.	None
◯	◯	◯	◯

3. Get the bus	at the corner	of Maple Street.	None
◯	◯	◯	◯

4. Can Fred and jack	come	to the movie?	None
◯	◯	◯	◯

Directions:
☐ Use words in the word box. ✔ each word as you use it.
☐ Write synonyms (words with about the same meaning) across→
☐ Write antonyms (words with opposite meanings) down↓.
☐ Draw ▨ in the unused squares on the puzzle to fill them in.

1. antonym for <u>below</u>
2. means the same as <u>gift</u>
3. synonym for <u>huge</u>
4. antonym for <u>win</u>
5. antonym for <u>heavy</u>
6. means the same as <u>happy</u>
7. synonym for <u>sick</u>
8. opposite of <u>day</u>
9. synonym for <u>fast</u>
10. opposite of <u>far</u>

Word Box

present	cheerful
light	night
ill	lose
quick	✔above
enormous	close

Healthy Information

Color the design according to the directions in
each statement. If you don't know what a word
means, look it up in a dictionary or health book.

☐ Color the five senses purple.

☐ Color good health habits green.

☐ Color body organs red.

☐ Color special types of
doctors blue.

☐ Color types of blood
vessels purple.

☐ Color diseases green.

☐ Color types of teeth red.

☐ Color bones blue.

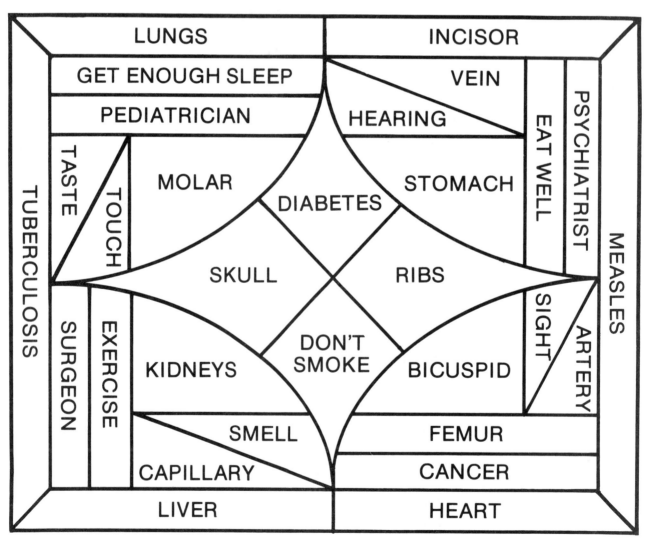

Brainwork! Choose one of the categories listed and write two more examples.

Wild Weather

Beginning with the top left corner, carefully follow the directions in each box. Follow the double lines to the next box, unless directed to do otherwise.

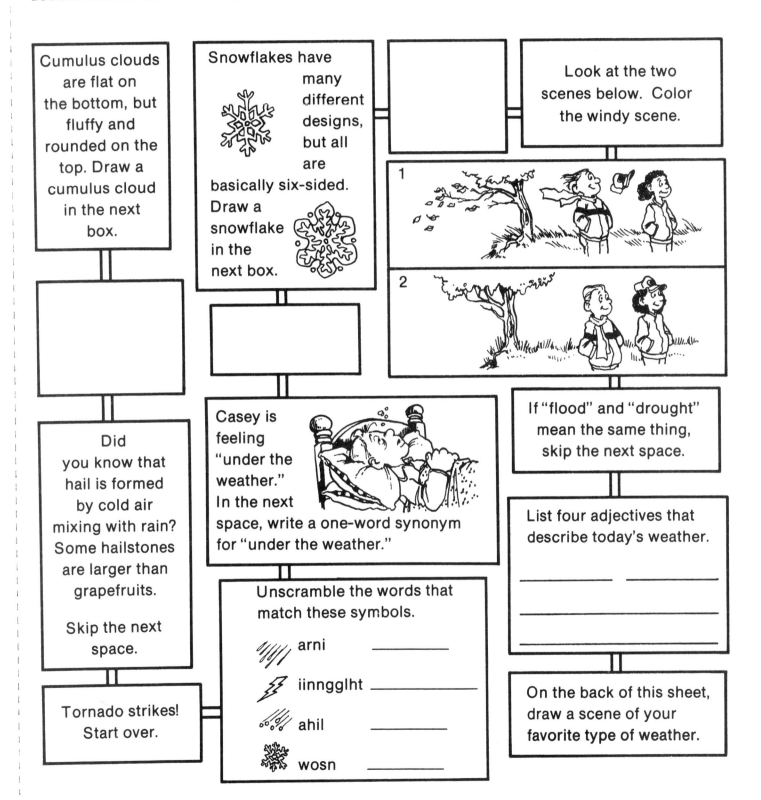

Cumulus clouds are flat on the bottom, but fluffy and rounded on the top. Draw a cumulus cloud in the next box.

Snowflakes have many different designs, but all are basically six-sided. Draw a snowflake in the next box.

Look at the two scenes below. Color the windy scene.

1

2

Did you know that hail is formed by cold air mixing with rain? Some hailstones are larger than grapefruits.

Skip the next space.

Casey is feeling "under the weather." In the next space, write a one-word synonym for "under the weather."

If "flood" and "drought" mean the same thing, skip the next space.

List four adjectives that describe today's weather.

_____ _____

_____

_____

Tornado strikes! Start over.

Unscramble the words that match these symbols.

arni _____

iinngglht _____

ahil _____

wosn _____

On the back of this sheet, draw a scene of your favorite type of weather.

Brainwork! Design a new box for the "Wild Weather" puzzle.

Amazing Animals

Canis rufus is the scientific name for an endangered animal that lives in the United States. Read the statements about animals. Follow the directions only if the first part of the statement is correct. When you finish, you will know the common name of the *canis rufus.* If you are unsure of a word, look it up in a dictionary.

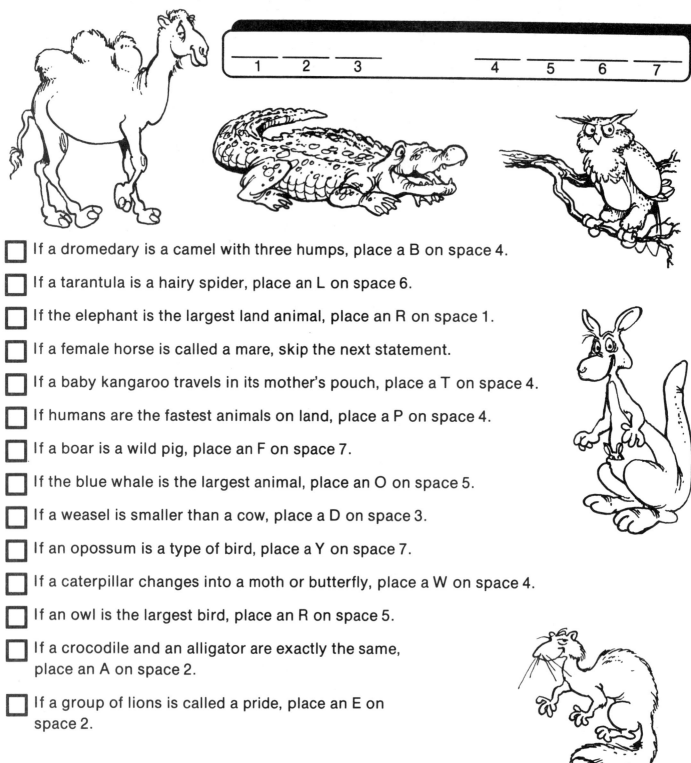

☐ If a dromedary is a camel with three humps, place a B on space 4.

☐ If a tarantula is a hairy spider, place an L on space 6.

☐ If the elephant is the largest land animal, place an R on space 1.

☐ If a female horse is called a mare, skip the next statement.

☐ If a baby kangaroo travels in its mother's pouch, place a T on space 4.

☐ If humans are the fastest animals on land, place a P on space 4.

☐ If a boar is a wild pig, place an F on space 7.

☐ If the blue whale is the largest animal, place an O on space 5.

☐ If a weasel is smaller than a cow, place a D on space 3.

☐ If an opossum is a type of bird, place a Y on space 7.

☐ If a caterpillar changes into a moth or butterfly, place a W on space 4.

☐ If an owl is the largest bird, place an R on space 5.

☐ If a crocodile and an alligator are exactly the same, place an A on space 2.

☐ If a group of lions is called a pride, place an E on space 2.

Brainwork! On the back of this sheet, write three animal facts.

FS-32018 Fourth Grade Activities

Where Are You Going?

Use this street map to answer the questions below.

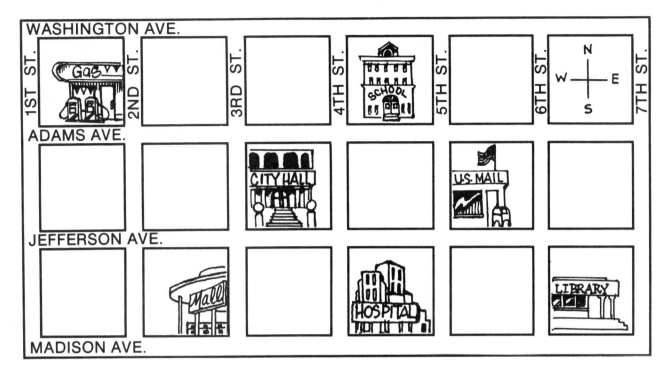

1. Your Aunt Gertrude just picked you up at the corner of
   7th St. and Madison Ave. You travel west four blocks and
   then north one block. What building are you near?

   _____

2. You and your cousin Abdul are leaving school. You walk
   a half block west, two blocks south, and then another
   block west. What building are you near?

   _____

3. After working at the gas station, Penelope Padilla rode
   her bike two blocks south, one block east, and three
   blocks north. She then rode two blocks east, three
   blocks south, and another block east. At which building
   did she end up?

   _____

4. Bob Bugaboo traveled one block north, then two blocks
   east and ended up at the post office. At which building
   did he begin?

   _____

5. Spot, a confused Dalmatian, wandered three blocks east,
   one block south, one block east, two blocks north, a half
   block west and ended up at school. At which corner did
   he begin?

   _____

Brainwork! Write directions for the shortest route from the school to the library. Then write
directions for a "scenic route."

         FS-32018 Fourth Grade Activities

Name _____

Directions:

☐ You live in the house at the corner of Peach Street and Second Street, **across from** ABC School. Put a * in that house.

☐ Your friend lives east of the library on the corner of Apple and Second Streets. Put an **X** on that house.

Which way? North, South, East, West?

☐ Hotel to ⟦*⟧. Go _____ .

☐ Tennis Court to Toy Store. Go _____ , then _____ .

☐ Library to Bank. Go _____ on Second Street then go _____ on Pear Street.

☐ High School to ⟦X⟧. Go _____ on Third Street, then _____ on Apple.

☐ What is at the corner of Peach and Third Streets? _____

☐ Make a dotted line to mark your path. You are at the Toy Store. Go South to Second Street. Go East to ⟦X⟧. Go North on Apple Street. Now go West on Third Street. Turn South on Pear Street. Go West on Park Drive. Go to the store on Park Drive between Peach and Pear Streets. What can you buy there?

Third Street

Hotel   Bank

Clothing Store

Park Drive

ABC School

Pear Street

Tennis Court

City Park

Plum Street

High School

Food Store

Toy Store

Library

Apple Street

Peach Street

Second Street

First Street

N
W — E
S

Name _____

Directions:
☐ Put a round table in the Southwest corner. ◯
☐ Put four chairs around the table. ∪
☐ Draw the sink between the closet and bookshelves. ◔
☐ The flag is in the Southeast corner. ⚑
☐ A clock is in the center of the West wall. ⏰
☐ The teacher's desk is under the clock. ▭
☐ Put a plant in the center of the round table. ▣
☐ A trash can is on the South side of the teacher's desk. ▽
☐ Another trash can is on the West side of the closet. ▽
☐ There are four rows of six desks each. They face towards the West wall of the classroom where the teacher sits. Make an **X** to show each desk. ✗
☐ Where would you like to sit in this classroom? Circle your desk. ⊗

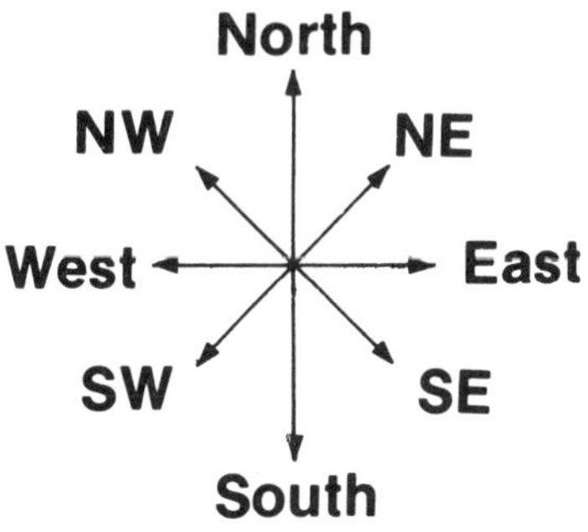

North
NW   NE
West ←→ East
SW   SE
South

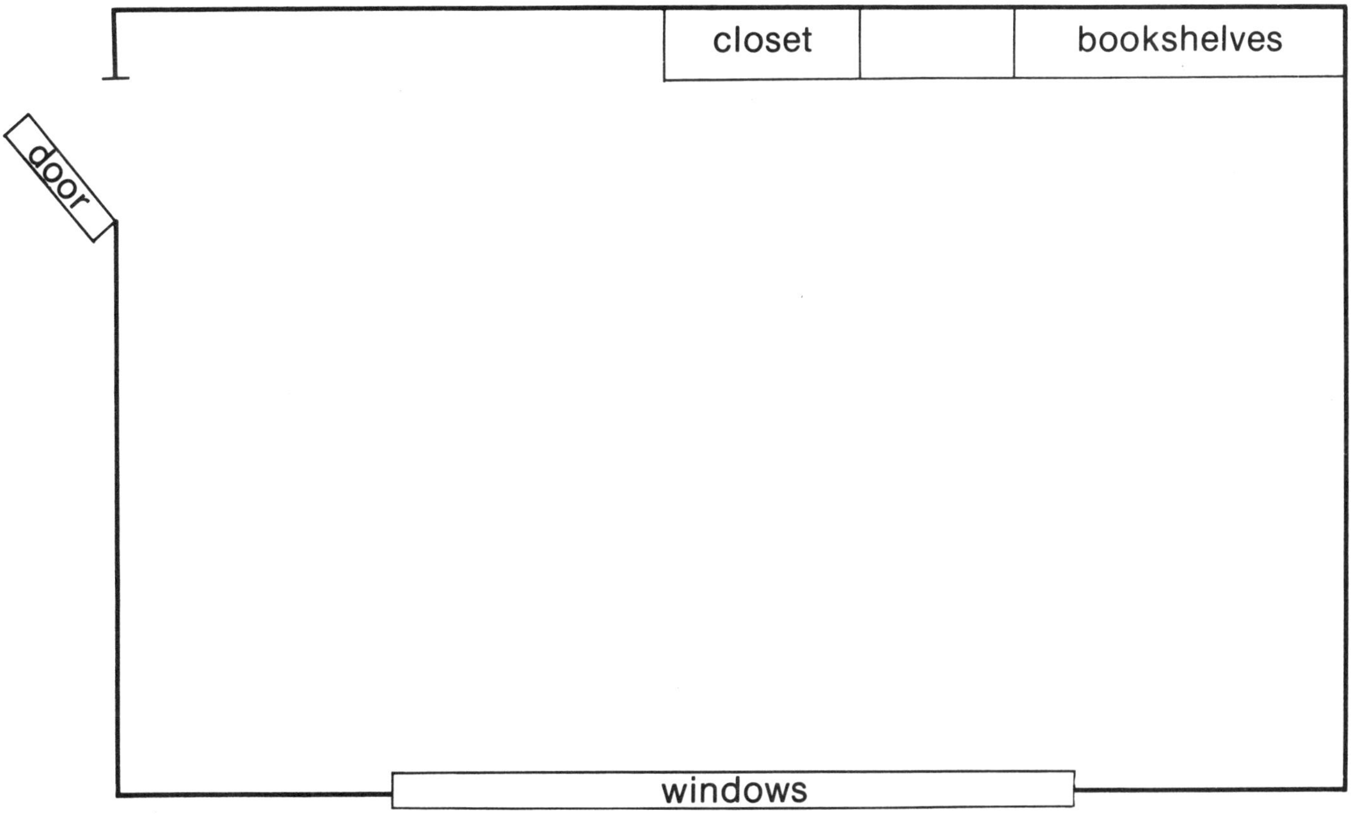

| | closet | | bookshelves |

door

windows

Name _____

Directions: Show the routes from city to city (● is a city).

☐ Draw a line to show the path from the northern California city to the state south of Utah. (_____)

☐ A jet goes from Washington to the state north of New Mexico. Then it goes to Utah and returns to Washington. Draw a dotted line to show its route.(_ _ _ _)

☐ Draw a wiggly line (〜〜) to show a jet trip from the state south of Montana to Nevada.

☐ Go from southern California to the state east of Arizona. Draw a curly line (eeee).

☐ Mark a path from the state north of California to the state north of Wyoming. Mark the path with a dash-dot line (—·—·—.).

☐ Number the eleven states in abc order.

_____ Washington
_____ Montana
_____ Oregon
_____ Idaho
_____ Wyoming
_____ California
_____ Nevada
_____ Utah
_____ Colorado
_1_ Arizona
_____ New Mexico

54

Shade Them In!

Follow the directions to shade in states on the map. Do not follow the directions if the first part of the statement is not correct.

☐ If Arizona is larger than Illinois, shade in Arizona.

☐ If Iowa is west of Utah, shade in Iowa.

☐ If Tennessee borders nine states, shade in Tennessee.

☐ If New Hampshire borders Massachusetts and Maine, shade in all three states.

☐ If both Nevada and Oregon border California, shade in California.

☐ If both Nebraska and Minnesota border Wyoming, shade in Wyoming.

☐ If Alaska and Hawaii do not border another state, shade them in.

☐ If Arkansas borders six states, shade in Florida.

☐ If Colorado is north of New Mexico, shade in Colorado.

☐ If Vermont borders Connecticut, shade in both states.

☐ If Idaho is larger than Ohio, shade in Idaho.

☐ If Michigan is smaller than Rhode Island, shade in Montana.

Brainwork! Write three more following directions statements for this map.

Where in the World?

Follow the directions below using an atlas, almanac, globe, or your social studies book for help.

☐ Label the oceans (Pacific, Atlantic, Indian, Arctic).

☐ Label the continents (North America, South America, Europe, Asia, Africa, Australia, Antarctica).

☐ Shade in the United States of America. Draw a star where your state is located.

☐ The equator is an imaginary line that divides the earth into northern and southern halves. Label the equator.

☐ The Mediterranean Sea is located between Europe and Africa, write "MS" where it is located.

☐ The Nile River, located in Africa, is the longest river in the world. Write "Nile River" along its path.

☐ Mt. Everest is the highest mountain in the world. Mark an "E" in the box that represents its location in Asia.

N
↑

Western Hemisphere   **Eastern Hemisphere**

Brainwork! Write directions for coloring each continent. Follow your own directions and color the map.

         FS-32018 Fourth Grade Activities

Famous Footsteps

Below are 16 famous footsteps and a not-so-famous one. The not-so-famous person was actually president of the United States for one day according to some historians. President Zachary Taylor's term was supposed to begin Sunday, March 4, 1849. For religious reasons, he waited to be sworn in as president until Monday. Therefore, the president of the Senate was in charge of the country for one day. To discover his name, carefully follow the directions below.

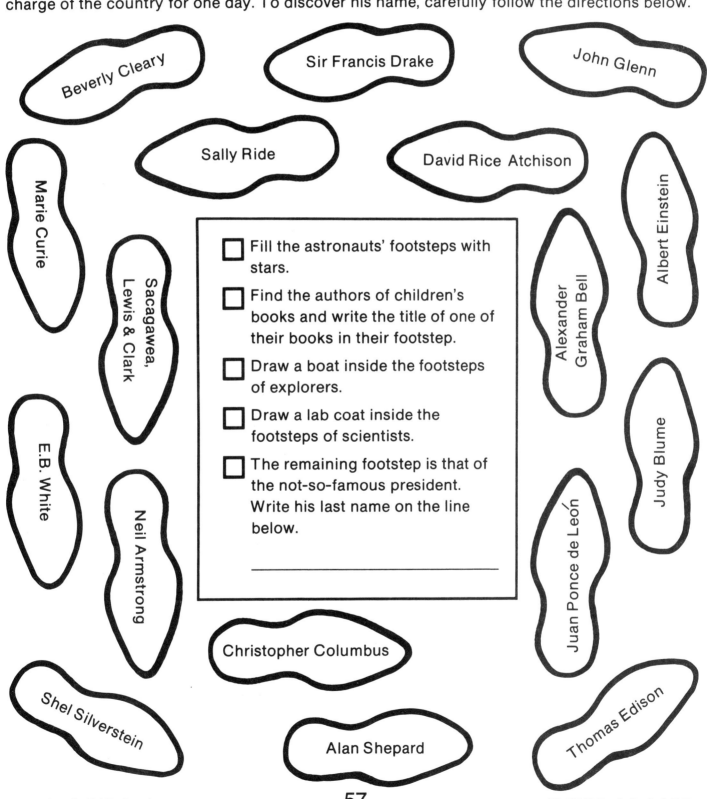

Beverly Cleary

Sir Francis Drake

John Glenn

Sally Ride

David Rice Atchison

Marie Curie

Albert Einstein

Sacagawea, Lewis & Clark

Alexander Graham Bell

☐ Fill the astronauts' footsteps with stars.

☐ Find the authors of children's books and write the title of one of their books in their footstep.

☐ Draw a boat inside the footsteps of explorers.

☐ Draw a lab coat inside the footsteps of scientists.

☐ The remaining footstep is that of the not-so-famous president. Write his last name on the line below.

_____

E.B. White

Judy Blume

Neil Armstrong

Juan Ponce de León

Christopher Columbus

Shel Silverstein

Alan Shepard

Thomas Edison

FS-32018 Fourth Grade Activities

Presidential Power!

Carefully follow the directions in each box. Follow the double lines to the next box unless directed to do otherwise.

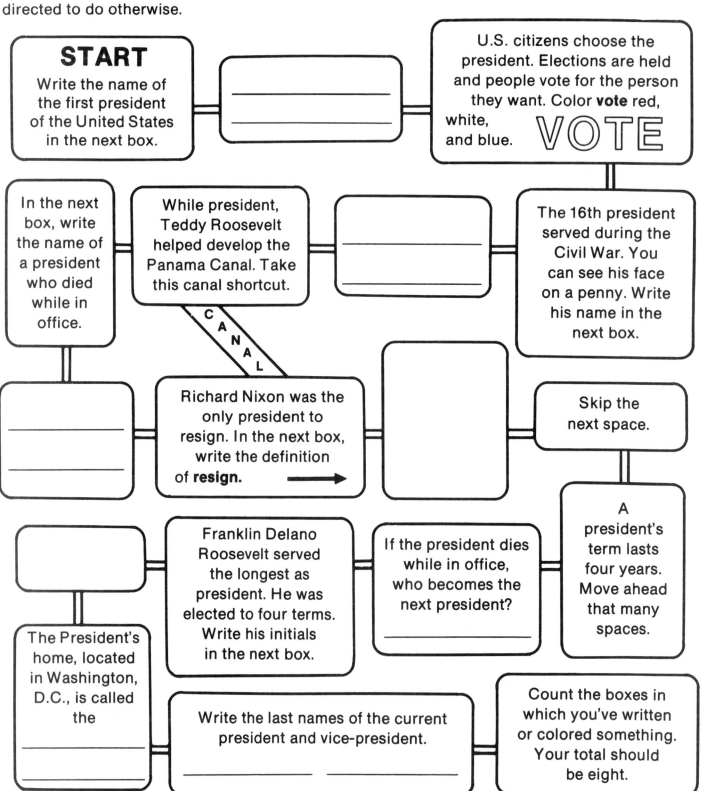

START
Write the name of the first president of the United States in the next box.

_____

U.S. citizens choose the president. Elections are held and people vote for the person they want. Color **vote** red, white, and blue. VOTE

In the next box, write the name of a president who died while in office.

While president, Teddy Roosevelt helped develop the Panama Canal. Take this canal shortcut.

_____

The 16th president served during the Civil War. You can see his face on a penny. Write his name in the next box.

_____

CANAL

Richard Nixon was the only president to resign. In the next box, write the definition of **resign.** ➝

Skip the next space.

The President's home, located in Washington, D.C., is called the
_____

Franklin Delano Roosevelt served the longest as president. He was elected to four terms. Write his initials in the next box.

If the president dies while in office, who becomes the next president?
_____

A president's term lasts four years. Move ahead that many spaces.

Write the last names of the current president and vice-president.

_____ _____

Count the boxes in which you've written or colored something. Your total should be eight.

Brainwork! In what year were you born? Find out who was president then.

FS-32018 Fourth Grade Activities

Citius, Altius, Fortius

"Citius, Altius, Fortius" is the motto of the Olympics. To discover what that means, read the statements below about Olympic, professional, and recreational sports. Use an encyclopedia if necessary. Follow the directions only if the first part of the statement is correct.

☐ If Martina Navratilova is a famous tennis player, place an I on space 8.

☐ If volleyball is played with a bat, place an A on space 13.

☐ If Nadia Comaneci and Mary Lou Retton were Olympic gymnasts, place an N on space 17.

☐ If roller skating is different than ice skating, place an A on space 2.

☐ If Jim Thorpe is a famous golfer, place an R on space 7.

☐ If the marathon is a long distance running race, place a T on spaces 4 and 14.

☐ If the Olympics are held every four years, place an E on spaces 5, 11, and 19.

☐ If bowling is played with a racket, place an S on space 15.

☐ If skiing takes place on snow or water, place an O on space 16.

☐ If athletes must be amateurs (unpaid) to compete in the Olympics, place a G on spaces 9 and 18.

☐ If Peggy Fleming, Dorothy Hamill, and Debi Thomas are famous ice skaters, place an R on spaces 6, 12, 15, and 20.

☐ If Larry Bird is a famous basketball player, place an F on 1.

☐ If there are Winter and Summer Olympics, place an H on spaces 7 and 10.

☐ If Jesse Owens won his Olympic medals in track and field events, place an S on spaces 3 and 13.

__	__	__	__	__	__	,	__	__	__	__	__	__	,	__	__	__	__	__	__	__	__
1	2	3	4	5	6		7	8	9	10	11	12		13	14	15	16	17	18	19	20

Guide Time

Guide words are listed at the top of each dictionary page. They tell us the first and last words we will find on that page.

Find each of the words listed below in your dictionary. Next to each word, write the guide words on the page where you found the word.

1. decrease _____

2. frame _____

3. hearth _____

4. incident _____

5. merchant _____

6. needle _____

7. otter _____

8. preview _____

9. salvage _____

10. symptom _____

11. trade _____

12. vessel _____

I never even noticed them!

apple

ascot

More Guide Words

Use your dictionary to find each word listed below. Write the guide words you find on the same page. Next, write the entry word that comes just before the word you are looking for.

EXAMPLE: <u>entry</u> <u>word</u> <u>to</u> <u>find</u>　　　<u>guide</u> <u>words</u>　　　<u>entry</u> <u>word</u> <u>before</u>

late　　　　　larder-lath　　　　latch string

	GUIDE WORDS	ENTRY WORD BEFORE
1. fish		
2. collide		
3. betray		
4. intersect		
5. lecture		
6. mimic		
7. partridge		
8. policy		
9. tag		
10. tablet		
11. shirk		
12. remnant		

Celebrity Sweepstakes

Put yourself in the dictionary. Write 5 words that would come before your name, and five that would follow it. Don't forget you need to use your last name.

EXAMPLE:
1. leg
2. letter
3. lily
4. lime
5. limit

Lincoln, Abraham
1. line
2. linear
3. link
4. linkage
5. lint

YOUR LIST
1. _____
2. _____
3. _____
4. _____
5. _____

_____
1. _____
2. _____
3. _____
4. _____
5. _____

Now put a friend or your teacher in the dictionary the same way.

1. _____
2. _____
3. _____
4. _____
5. _____

_____
1. _____
2. _____
3. _____
4. _____
5. _____

I'll do Wilma.

Repeat

The dictionary respells words to help you pronounce the ones you don't know. Find each word below in the dictionary. Write the respelling. Be sure to leave space between the syllables and show the accent marks.

EXAMPLE: balloon (bə lün′)

1. loaf _____
2. illegal _____
3. extend _____
4. design _____
5. desire _____
6. caret _____
7. caribou _____
8. bewitch _____
9. appeal _____
10. better _____

> Guess which one I am!

Now, rewrite the paragraph below. Replace the respelling with the real word it stands for.

Baseball is my (fā′vər it) game. I (prak′tis) whenever I have a (spâr) (min′it). I (hōp) that someday I'll be a (fā məs) (stär). Dad (sed) he would get me a (nü) (gluv) for my (bérth′ dā). I can hardly (wāt) for that (dā).

_____

_____

_____

_____

_____

Play That One Again

Use your dictionary to help you rewrite each word below showing its pronunciation. Don't forget to mark those vowels where needed. Next to each word, write the number of syllables you have shown in the word.

One, two...

EXAMPLE: beat · b̄et 1

1. nonsense _____ __
2. induction _____ __
3. formless* _____ __
4. crow _____ __
5. cucumber _____ __
6. fellow _____ __
7. harvest _____ __
8. interstate _____ __
9. medicated _____ __
10. meaty _____ __
11. react _____ __
12. rowdy _____ __

*Use the word <u>formless</u> in a sentence. (be sure to check its meaning.)

_____

_____

What does the suffix <u>less</u> mean in the word formless?

_____

Game Words

Write one game each of these things might be used in.

Use each word in a sentence.

> **EXAMPLE:** puck　　hockey　　**We used a puck in our hockey game.**

1. set _____
2. wicket _____
3. iron _____
4. touchdown _____
5. goalie _____
6. infield _____
7. field goal _____
8. trump _____
9. Ace _____
10. balk _____
11. quiver _____
12. basket _____
13. down _____
14. love _____

What's What

Some words may be pronounced more than one way. Look for each of these words and write both respellings.

EXAMPLE: rodeo   rō′dē ō   or   rō dā′ō

1. catsup _____

2. cerebral _____

3. detail _____

4. consort _____

5. contrite _____

6. cooperative _____

7. bouquet _____

8. adult _____

9. syrup _____

10. substitute _____

Now, try to pronounce **each** word in the two ways you have shown. Put a circle around the respelling that shows the way you say the word, or have heard it said most often.

Short Stuff

Dictionaries help us spell and understand abbreviations. Find each abbreviation in your dictionary. Write the meaning.

1. C.O.D. _____

2. Col. _____

3. bu. _____

4. bdl. _____

5. B.C. _____

6. Aug. _____

7. ans. _____

8. a.m. or A.M. _____

9. alt. _____

10. Ala. _____

Use at least three of the above abbreviations in sentences. Write them on the lines below. Underline the abbreviations you have used.

_____

_____

_____

_____

_____

_____

More Short Stuff

Find these abbreviations in your dictionary. Use each one in a sentence.

1. AEC _____
2. Adv. _____
3. A.D. _____
4. BA or AB _____
5. cu. _____
6. doz. _____
7. D.P. _____
8. ct. _____
9. Dr. _____
10. D.S.T. _____

Can you find other abbreviations in your dictionary? List two or more and tell what they mean.

_____

_____

_____

_____

_____

Picture Perfect Clues

Sometimes dictionaries contain pictures that help us understand the meanings of words. Find the words below and draw a picture that shows the meaning of each word below.

1. conning tower

2. coot

3. cope

4. cupola

5. decanter

6. derby

7. dibble

8. dirigible

9. discus

10. curlew

Scavenger Hunt

Hunt through your dictionary to find each answer. Check the underlined word.

1. Why can't an animal be a large <u>mite</u>?

_____

2. Why can't you fight a <u>Warsaw</u>?

_____

3. Why can't you curl your hair in <u>rivulets</u>?

_____

4. Why don't cows graze in a <u>pastern</u>?

_____

5. Why can't you get things to stick on <u>paste board</u>?

_____

6. Can you hear something <u>grackle</u>? __ why?

_____

7. Tell one job a <u>gaucho</u> could do.

_____

8. Why can't you <u>gauge</u> out a hole?

_____

9. Why isn't a <u>carillon</u> a good car?

_____

10. Why don't we find cars in a <u>carmine</u>?

_____

I've had quite a problem with mites this year.

Gone Hunting

Hunt through the dictionary to find out **what you would do** with each of these things or people. Write **your answer on** the line.

EXAMPLE: clarinet — play it

1. bannock _____

2. incisor _____

3. carter _____

4. gondola _____

5. dovecote _____

6. ensign _____

7. flask _____

8. goblet _____

9. gooseberry _____

10. haversack _____

11. Indian club _____

Something New

Find the underlined words below in your dictionary. Read each meaning of the word. Now write a sentence using the word with a different meaning than that in the printed sentence. You may use a different form of the word.

EXAMPLE: He was on the last leg of his journey. The table has legs.

1. Did he <u>exercise</u> today?

   _____

2. Did you see the <u>flag</u> flap in the breeze?

   _____

3. They saw the Chinese <u>junk</u>.

   _____

4. They climbed the <u>flight</u> of stairs.

   _____

5. He saw a light <u>flash</u>.

   _____

6. He hoped for a good <u>fortune</u>.

   _____

7. He committed a <u>foul</u> during the game.

   _____

8. They walked through the <u>gallery</u>.

   _____

9. They <u>introduced</u> a new food at the show.

   _____

10. Did you <u>join</u> the club?

    _____

11. Your fingers have <u>joints</u>.

    _____

12. The boys were <u>game</u> for anything.

    _____

The Same But Different

Two or more words may be spelled the same way. *Well, what do you know!*

EXAMPLE: till 1 (til) until
till 2 (til) cultivate; plow
till 3 (til) a small drawer for money

Use your dictionary to find the different words that are spelled like those below. Write one meaning for each different word.

A. batter 1. _____
2. _____
3. _____

B. baste 1. _____
2. _____

C. bat 1. _____
2. _____
3. _____

D. ash 1. _____
2. _____

E. cue 1. _____
2. _____

F. cricket 1. _____
2. _____
3. _____

G. junk 1. _____
2. _____

Special Meanings

Some words have special meanings. By looking for the word dust, we find special meanings such as: bite the dust, lick the dust, or shake the dust off one's feet.

Look for the most important word in each expression below. Find that word in the dictionary. (If it isn't listed, try a different word. The first few were underlined for you.) Write the meaning.

1. catch one's <u>eye</u>_____

2. keep one's <u>head</u> _____

3. take <u>heart</u> _____

4. rack one's brain _____

5. bury the hatchet _____

6. follow in one's footstep_____

7. out of sorts_____

8. crocodile tears _____

9. see eye to eye _____

10. an eye for an eye _____

What's the Beat?

When we pronounce a word with more than one syllable, we usually accent (say with more force) one of the syllables. An accent mark (′) is placed after that syllable. Try to mark the accented syllable in each word below, then use your dictionary to check your work.

> **EXAMPLE:** Play ′ ground

1. learn er
2. flow er
3. di vide
4. dis tinct
5. cen ter
6. cen ti pede
7. car rot
8. car na tion
9. car toon
10. car ton
11. bi cy cle
12. ap point
13. ap ple
14. ap pear
15. a ble

doo dah dah dee dee dee!

thump

tap tap

FS-32018 Fourth Grade Activities

Multiple Meanings

Look at the meanings of each word. Put the number of the meaning used in each sentence below. You may use the same number twice.

> **good (gud)**   1. excellent   2. well-behaved   3. right
>   4. desirable   5. satisfying   6. pleasant   7. kind, friendly
>   8. real: genuine   9. benefit

_5_ A. The dinner was good.

_____ B. What good will it do?

_____ C. He received a good grade.

_____ D. Say a good word for me.

_____ E. It is good money.

_____ F. He is a good boy.

_____ G. That is a good book for children to read.

_____ H. That answer is good.

_____ I. Have a good time.

Let's see.

> **dispatch (dis pach)**   1. send off for a purpose   2. send a letter etc.
>   3. A written message   4. get something done promptly   5. finish off

_____ J. The dispatch arrived.

_____ K. He dispatched the telegram.

_____ L. He dispatched a messenger to inform the President.

_____ M. She did the job with dispatch.

_____ N. They dispatched the cake.

What's He Talking About

The dictionary shows pronunciation (the way to say) of each word. Look at the respellings in parenthesis ( ) below. Write the word, spelling it correctly. The pronunciation key at the front of your dictionary will help you.

1. Do you know how to (də vīd′)? _____

2. Did he (kəm plēt′) his work? _____

3. She put (ī′ə dīn) on the cut. _____

4. The (jür i) found him guilty. _____

5. Mom is at the (mär′ kit) _____

6. A (pla tō′) is a plain in the mountains. _____

7. Put lots of food on my (plāt). _____

8. (Rō) the boat to shore. _____

9. They sat on the (san′ di) shore. _____

10. I feel (sik). _____

11. Take your (tern). _____

12. I (wil) do the job. _____

What's going on?

....Try reading the instructions.

77

Root Words

To find the meaning of a word, we must look for the root word. Example: To find the meaning of painted, we would look for paint.

Write the root word in each word below. Be sure to put in any letters that were taken out when an ending was added. Look for the root word in the dictionary and write the first meaning.

1. appointed _____ 1. _____

2. bigger _____ 1. _____

3. composing _____ 1. _____

4. dabbling _____ 1. _____

5. discouraged _____ 1. _____

6. divinities _____ 1. _____

7. finances _____ 1. _____

8. gassing _____ 1. _____

9. generalities_____ 1. _____

10. gasped_____ 1. _____

11. goodies _____ 1. _____

12. leakiest _____ 1. _____

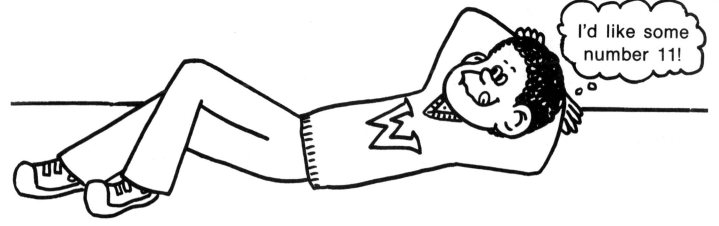

I'd like some number 11!

Dictionary Merits*

syllables
pronounce
quickly
meanings
accented
spell
guide
long
short
entry

A. Each page in the dictionary has 1 (down) _____ words at the top to help us find or locate words 2 (down) _____ .

B. We can find one or more 3 _____ for words in the dictionary.

C. We can learn to divide words into 4 (down) _____ .

D. Each word that is defined (meaning is given) in a dictionary is called an 5 (down) _____ word.

E. Dictionaries help us 6 _____ and 7 (down) _____ words.

F. We can tell if words have 8 _____ or 9 _____ sounds.

G. We can even learn which syllable is 10 _____ (has the strongest sound).

*Bonus:

Find this word in your dictionary and write the meanings. **Merit** _____

_____

Name _____ **Date** _____

Read the stories. Circle the **best** conclusion for each one.

---

1. "The secret map says we should go four paces to the right. Then we walk ten paces straight ahead and go past the tree," said Sam.
   "Then we dig!" said Bob.
   Sam and Bob are probably:
   a. taking a walk   b. hunting for treasure   c. visiting friends

---

2. Jim Grant sat in the rocket ship. He was buckled into his seat and waiting for the countdown.
   "10-9-8-7-6-5-4-3-2-1-Blast-off!" The rocket rose from its launching pad and headed into outer space.
   Jim is probably:
   a. an airline pilot
   b. a visitor from Mars
   c. an astronaut

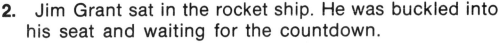

3. The bird began to build a nest. She used twigs and leaves as building materials.
   Next she will probably:
   a. lay her eggs   b. hatch her eggs   c. fly away

4. "Groan! I shouldn't have stayed up so late last night," Ann said. "But that scary creature feature about the two-headed duck was really good. I wish I could just get my eyes open."
   Ann is probably:
   a. trying to wake up
   b. walking home from school
   c. leaving a movie theater.

--- **Thinking Time** ---

Read the next two questions. Answer them on the back of this paper.

1. Imagine you were an astronaut. Where would you go? What new forms of life would you discover on your trip?

2. It has many eyes but it does not see. It grows under the ground. It goes well with hamburgers. What is it?

    80   FS-32018 Fourth Grade Activities

Read the stories. Circle the **best** conclusion for each one.

---

1. These people use refrigerators to keep their food from freezing. It is so cold where they live that food will freeze if left outside.

   You can guess these people are called:
   a. Chinese   b. Arabs   c. Eskimos

---

2. Mary found an old mug in the cupboard. "I wonder why Mother put this mug away?" Mary asked. She washed it out. Then she put some tomato juice in it and began drinking. Mary looked at her blouse. "Now I know why we never use it," she said.

   You can guess:
   a. The mug had a crack in it.
   b. The mug was dirty.
   c. The mug had no handle.

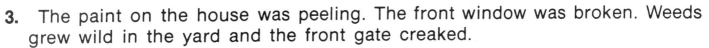

---

3. The paint on the house was peeling. The front window was broken. Weeds grew wild in the yard and the front gate creaked.

   You can guess the house was:
   a. new   b. beautiful   c. deserted

4. Bernie has strange tastes. He loves rattlesnake meat and chocolate-covered ants. His favorite food is a fruit. When Bernie eats it, he says, "Here's to Sour Power!"

   You can guess his favorite food is a:
   a. banana
   b. lemon
   c. plum

--- **Thinking Time** ---

Read the next two questions. Answer them on the back of this paper.

1. What happened to Mary's blouse in the second story?

2. Make up a story about the **people who** lived in the house in the third story.

Name _____ **Date** _____

Read the stories. Circle the **best** conclusion for each one.

---

1. The rain poured down for days. Every day the river rose higher and higher.
    If it did not stop raining soon, there would be:
    a. a hurricane   b. a flood   c. an earthquake

---

2. Tom told Sara to meet him at his house after school. When Sara reached his house, she knocked on the door. There was no answer so she just walked inside. It was dark in the room. As Sara turned on the lights she heard several people yell, "Surprise!"

    You can guess it was:
    a. a robber
    b. Sara's birthday
    c. the last day of school

---

3. Fred stood at the top of the snow-covered hill and leaned on his poles.
    He was all set to:
    a. ski   b. skate   c. bobsled

4. Pat put $.75 in his pocket for lunch money. When he got to school he ran into several of his friends. He stopped to talk to them for awhile.
    "Hey! I just found three quarters on the ground!" his friend Jack yelled.

    You can guess:
    a. The money had been lying there for several days.
    b. The money belonged to the school nurse.
    c. Pat's pocket had a hole in it.

Thinking Time

Read the next two questions. Answer them on the back of this paper.

1. What might happen to a dam during a flood? Describe what would happen to the houses in the area.

2. What is wrong with this story? Marsha took off her skates and put on her shoes. Then she went skating.

Read the stories. Circle the **best** conclusion for each one.

1. Matt was in the kitchen making dinner. Sally was in the living room watching the evening news on TV.

    It is probably:
    a. 7:30 a.m.   b. 12:00 p.m.   c. 6:00 p.m.

2. Andy found a basketball in an empty lot. "This is great! All it needs is some air," he said. He pumped it up and began bouncing it. "Hey, this ball is no good," Andy said.

    You can guess the ball:
    a. was the wrong color
    b. had a hole in it
    c. was too small

3. Polly went for a swim in the ocean. Suddenly she noticed a large fin sticking out of the water. It began circling her.

    You can guess the fin belonged to a:
    a. whale   b. swordfish   c. shark

4. As Paul watched the movie, his eyes grew bigger and bigger. He gulped several times. His hands shook and were icy cold. During certain parts, he put his hands over his eyes.

    You can guess the movie was:
    a. funny
    b. scary
    c. sad

──────── **Thinking Time** ────────

Read the next two questions. Answer them on the back of this paper.

1. In the second story, what do you think Andy did with the ball?
2. What do you think Polly did in the third story?

Read the stories. Circle the **best** conclusion for each one.

1. It is spring. The orange tree in our backyard is covered with white blossoms.
   You can guess that the tree will soon:
   a. lose its leaves   b. have red blossoms   c. bear fruit

2. Mordor was a visitor from Mars. He had four ears and three arms. One day Peggy walked up behind him.
   "Hello, Peggy," Mordor said without turning around.
   "How did you know it was me?" Peggy asked.
   You can guess that Mordor:
   a. had eyes in the back of his head
   b. was Peggy's father
   c. could only see things in front of him

3. Brian entered the bubblegum-blowing contest. He blew a huge bubble. It got bigger and bigger. He continued blowing. It got even bigger.
   You can guess that the bubble:
   a. grew bigger than Brian   b. floated away   c. burst

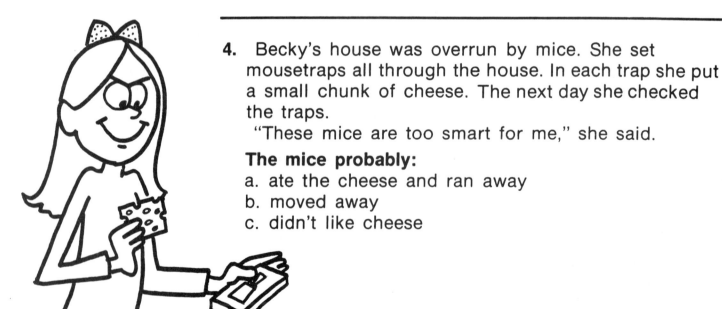

4. Becky's house was overrun by mice. She set mousetraps all through the house. In each trap she put a small chunk of cheese. The next day she checked the traps.
   "These mice are too smart for me," she said.
   The mice probably:
   a. ate the cheese and ran away
   b. moved away
   c. didn't like cheese

————————————— **Thinking Time** —————————————

Read the next two questions. Answer them on the back of this paper.

1. Draw a picture of Mordor.

2. Make up a conversation between two mice. Imagine they live at Becky's house.

Read the stories. Circle the **best** conclusion for each one.

1.   Tom looked out the window. "It looks like a great day for kite flying," he said.

You can guess it is probably:
a. sunny   b. windy   c. cloudy

2.   Jack was late for school. He dressed quickly and dashed out the door. When he got to school he sat down at his desk. He glanced down at his feet and his face turned bright red.

You can guess:
a. He had worn his best pair of socks.
b. His socks were too big.
c. Each sock was a different color.

3.   First, Mike polished his shoes until they shone. Then, he shaved and patted his face with after-shave lotion. Finally, he put on his new black suit.

Mike is probably going to:
a. a dance   b. the movies   c. a baseball game

4.   Jane was going to take a bath. She turned on the faucets and began running the bath water.
   "Jane, can you help me a minute?" her mother asked. Jane helped her mother set the table for dinner. Then she looked up at the ceiling. She quickly ran upstairs.

You can guess:
a. The ceiling had a hole in it.
b. The bath tub was overflowing.
c. The ceiling light had gone out.

──────────────── **Thinking Time** ────────────────

Read the next two questions. Answer them on the back of this paper.

1. How old do you think Mike is in the third story? Why?

2. What will happen next in the fourth story?

Read the stories. Circle the **best** conclusion for each one.

---

1. He is old, but stands tall. He has a white beard and wears a red, white and blue outfit. He is a symbol of America to people all over the world.
    You can guess he is:
    a. George Washington   b. Uncle Sam   c. Abraham Lincoln

---

2. Debbie had just bought a new sports car. She decided to go for a drive. Debbie turned on the motor and put her foot on the gas. After driving just a short way, she heard a siren behind her.
    You can guess that Debbie:
    a. was driving too fast
    b. had run out of gas
    c. didn't have her seat belt on

---

3. The rain has ended. Now the sun is coming out. The raindrops are sparkling in the sunlight.
    If we are lucky we may see:
    a. a rainbow   b. a pot of gold   c. stars

4. Dad checked everything in the car. "We have sleeping bags, a lantern, a tent, firewood and food. Looks like we're ready to go."
    He looked once more and then he smiled. "There's only one problem. There's no room for us!"
    The family in this story is probably:
    a. going sailing
    b. going on a picnic
    c. going camping

--- **Thinking Time** ---

Read the next two questions. Answer them on the back of this paper.

1. Imagine you are going on a picnic. What are some things you will need to take along?

2. In the second story, Debbie hears a siren. Who is following her? What will happen to her?

FS-32018 Fourth Grade Activities

Read the stories. Circle the **best** conclusion for each one.

---

1. Amanda was reading an exciting story. It was about a woman who had magic powers. She could fly and turn carrots into gold.

   Amanda was probably reading a:
   a. fairy tale   b. true story   c. history book

---

2. Peggy piled meat, lettuce, cheese and tomatoes on top of some bread. "This needs some mayonnaise," she said. She found a jar marked mayonnaise in the refrigerator. "Yuck, this tastes awful!" she said. Just then Roger started looking in the refrigerator.
   "Hey, have you seen my jar of paste?" he asked.

   You can guess that:
   a. The mayonnaise jar had paste in it.
   b. The mayonnaise was spoiled.
   c. Peggy put too much salt on the sandwich.

---

3. Nat looked out the window. He saw a jet take off. Then he saw a small plane land on the airfield. Meanwhile, another plane moved down the runway.

   Nat is probably at the:
   a. airport   b. space center   c. bus station

---

4. "The trees are so thick, I can hardly see!" Bob said.
   "I think that hanging vine is really a snake!" Pam screamed.
   "Shh! I hear a lion growling!" Sam whispered.

   They are probably:
   a. in the mountains
   b. in the jungle
   c. near the ocean

Thinking Time

Read the next two questions. Answer them on the back of this paper.

1. What should Peggy have done in the second story?
2. In the third story what do you think Nat is about to do?

        FS-32018 Fourth Grade Activities

Read the stories. Circle the **best** conclusion for each one.

---

1. Ben looked at the calendar on his bedroom wall. The date June 16th was circled in red. "Only one more week until the last day!" he said happily.
   You can guess June 16th is:
   a. the last day of vacation   b. the last day of school   c. Ben's birthday

---

2. Becky had studied very hard for the history test. Mrs. Brown, her teacher, passed out the tests to the students. "Remember," she said, "the test is on Chapters 6-9." "Oh, no!" Becky cried.
   You can guess Becky:
   a. studied the wrong chapters
   b. thinks she will do well on the test
   c. is in the wrong room

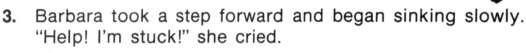

3. Barbara took a step forward and began sinking slowly. "Help! I'm stuck!" she cried.
   Barbara had probably:
   a. fallen into a hole   b. gotten caught in quicksand   c. fallen into a stream

4. George bought two pieces of candy. He popped both pieces into his mouth and began chewing them. The candy stuck to his teeth. He chewed harder. Now the candy stuck to his tongue.
   "Hi, George. How are you?" Rob asked.
   "Mmmfhmm!" George said.
   George was probably eating:
   a. taffy
   b. chocolate bars
   c. sour balls

Thinking Time

Read the next two questions. Answer them on the back of this paper.

1. Name three kinds of candy that take a long time to eat.

2. Imagine you are taking a trip through a jungle. What are some things you will have to watch out for?

Name _____ **Date** _____

Read the stories. Circle the **best** conclusion for each one.

---

1. It looks like a flying eggbeater. It can move up, down, sideways or hover in the air.

   You can guess it is:
   a. a jet   b. an airplane   c. a helicopter

---

2. It was a wet, cold morning. Paul put on his bearskin and reached for his club. He crawled out of his cave. He could see a huge dinosaur in the distance.
   "Paul, it's time to get up. You'll be late for school," his mother said.

   Paul was probably:
   a. dreaming
   b. a real caveman
   c. lost

3. The sap from this tree is used to make many different things. Some of the things are tires, balls and rain boots.

   You can guess this tree is called a:
   a. metal tree   b. rubber tree   c. leather tree

4. Bob decided today was a good day to try his experiment. He took an egg from the refrigerator and went outside. Then he cracked the egg over the sidewalk. It began to fry as if it were in a pan on the stove.

   It was probably a _____ day.
   a. warm
   b. very hot
   c. cold

Thinking Time

Read the next two questions. Answer them on the back of this paper.

1. Trees have many valuable uses. Name three.

2. What's wrong with this story? Sally had to clean the house. She washed all the dishes. Then she unmade all the beds. Finally, she swept the floors.

Read the stories. Circle the **best** conclusion for each one.

1. "Gee, I wish I were like Jeff," said Nan. "He really has a green thumb. All his plants do well. I guess I have a brown thumb."

   Nan is probably _____ gardening.
   a. good at   b. not good at   c. not interested in

2. Elaine wanted to get the spy ring that unlocked secret messages. For two weeks she ate Zowie cereal every day.

   You can guess Elaine:
   a. loved Zowie cereal
   b. had to mail in cereal boxtops to get the ring
   c. only had cereal in the house

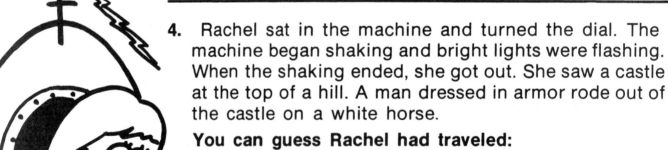

3. Tim was thinking about a round, flat pie. It was covered with tomato sauce, cheese and sausage. Tim went to the phone and started dialing a number.

   You can guess he:
   a. ordered a pizza   b. called a friend   c. made his own pizza

4. Rachel sat in the machine and turned the dial. The machine began shaking and bright lights were flashing. When the shaking ended, she got out. She saw a castle at the top of a hill. A man dressed in armor rode out of the castle on a white horse.

   You can guess Rachel had traveled:
   a. into the past
   b. into the future
   c. to modern-day England

—— Thinking Time ——

Read the next two questions. Answer them on the back of this paper.

1. Can you make a special kind of food? Describe how you prepare it step-by-step.

2. Paul bought some hay and oats at the feed store. What kind of animal do you think Paul owns?

Name _____ Date _____

Read the stories. Circle the **best** conclusion for each one.

---

1. "What a day! First I get a sore throat so I can't roar. Then an elephant steps on my paw. I don't feel much like the King of the Jungle today!"
You can guess I am a:
a. tiger   b. lion   c. bear

---

2. Jeff was practicing a new trick. First he put a tablecloth on the table. Next he set the table with plates and cups. Then he tried to whisk the cloth off the table without disturbing the cups or plates.
Jeff probably:
a. breaks a lot of cups and plates
b. gets the trick right the first time
c. has a very happy mother

---

3. Mark and Sue visited a strange planet. There were ten-foot carrot trees. Enormous spinach leaves were used to make roofs. Potatoes were as large as Earth's pumpkins.
You can guess this planet was called:
a. Fruitworld   b. Spinachoid   c. Vegetableania

4. "On your mark, get set, go!" Sally, Lucy and Dana began running at top speed. When they crossed the finish line they were all panting. Their running times were: Dana at 2 minutes, Lucy at 1 minute 30 seconds and Sally at 1 minute 32 seconds.
You can tell _____ won the race.
a. Dana
b. Lucy
c. Sally

--- Thinking Time ---

Read the next two questions. Answer them on the back of this paper.

1. What is your favorite trick? How long did it take you to learn it?

2. What's wrong with this story? Pam just turned twelve. This morning she dressed and ate breakfast. Then she drove her car to school.

Read the stories. Circle the **best** conclusion for each one.

1. He travels all over the country. Sometimes he carries loads of fruits and vegetables to market. Other times he carries lumber or gasoline.

You can guess he is a:

a. policeman   b. truck driver   c. farmer

2. Jack and Jean wanted to go to the zoo. When they got into Jack's car, he looked at the dashboard. "Uh-oh," Jack said. "I think we'll have to walk to the park instead."

You can guess:
a. Jack had forgotten his keys.
b. The car was out of gas.
c. The zoo was closed.

3. Roger and John built a sand castle at the beach. It had four towers, a drawbridge and a moat. After they left, the tide came in.

When they returned the next day, the castle:

a. was gone   b. was floating in the ocean   c. was still there

4. Gale and her family went on a camping trip. There was a sign posted at the campgrounds. It said: Watch Out For Bears. The family unpacked their things and went for a walk. When they returned, they discovered all their food was gone. Their tent was ripped apart, too.

You can guess:
a. There had been a big thunderstorm.
b. Squirrels had wandered through the camp.
c. Bears had visited the camp.

───── **Thinking Time** ─────

Read the next two questions. Answer them on the back of this paper.

1. What should the family in the fourth story have done to protect their food and tent?

2. If you had one wish, what would you wish for?

Read the stories. Circle the **best** conclusion for each one.

---

1. This cartoon hero loves carrots. He also loves to play jokes on people. His favorite saying is, "What's up, Doc?"

You can guess he is:

a. Mickey Mouse   b. Daffy Duck   c. Bugs Bunny

---

2. All of Susie's toys were packed into a big box. Her suitcase was filled with clothes. Her mother had just finished putting all the dishes and pans into crates. Just then a big truck pulled up in the driveway.

You can guess Susie and her family are:

a. getting ready for a trip
b. moving to a new city
c. having a garage sale

---

3. My dog Lad is very friendly. However, he doesn't realize how big and strong he is. He is even bigger than I am. When I come home from school, Lad dashes straight towards me.

You can guess he:

a. knocks me down   b. sits quietly   c. jumps over me

4. My friend Jake works at the circus. Sometimes he shows off at home. When he washes the dishes he balances a teacup on his nose. Then he tosses the dishes from one hand to another. When Jake washes dishes, his mother always closes her eyes.

You can guess Jake is a:

a. lion tamer
b. tightrope walker
c. juggler

——— Thinking Time ———

Read the next two questions. Answer them on the back of this paper.

1. Who is your favorite cartoon hero? Why?

2. How old do you think Lad's owner might be? Why?

Name _____ **Date** _____

Read the stories. Circle the **best** conclusion for each one.

---

1. They are very hard workers. They can carry objects several times larger than they are. One of them can even carry a huge breadcrumb all by himself!

   They are probably:

   a. horses   b. people   c. ants

---

2. Thump! Dad and Mom were awakened in the middle of the night. Someone was in the house! Dad took a flashlight and crept downstairs. As he walked through the kitchen, the cat dashed out the door.

   The noise was probably caused by:

   a. a robber
   b. the cat
   c. a dog

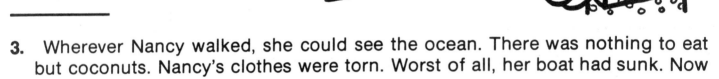

3. Wherever Nancy walked, she could see the ocean. There was nothing to eat but coconuts. Nancy's clothes were torn. Worst of all, her boat had sunk. Now she could never leave!

   Nancy is probably:

   a. on a ship   b. on an island   c. lost in the woods

4. My dog Rover can do a lot of tricks. When I call him, he rolls over. When I tell him to roll over, he goes to sleep. His best trick of all is standing still.

   This year at the dog show, Rover will probably:
   a. win many prizes
   b. not win any prizes
   c. do several new tricks

————— Thinking Time —————

Read the next two questions. Answer them on the back of this paper.

1. In the second story the word "thump" tells us something happened. What do you think it was?

2. Nancy has a problem in the third story. What would you do if you were her?

     94   FS-32018 Fourth Grade Activities

Name _____ **Date** _____

Read the stories. Circle the **best** conclusion for each one.

1. Carl found some nails in a field. He could tell they had been there for quite awhile.

   The nails were probably:
   a. shiny   b. black   c. rusty

2. Ray waxed and polished his car. Next he watered the lawn. Finally, he washed all the windows on his house from the outside. Just then dark clouds began to gather in the sky. "I should have known this would happen!" he groaned.

   You can guess:
   a. It will rain.
   b. There will be an earthquake.
   c. It will snow.

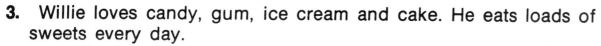

3. Willie loves candy, gum, ice cream and cake. He eats loads of sweets every day.

   You can guess Willie:
   a. doesn't have good teeth   b. is very strong   c. is very tall

4. Connie sawed some boards in two. Then she hammered the boards into the wooden frame. Soon she would be ready to put up the roof.

   You can guess Connie is building a:
   a. bed
   b. house
   c. ten-story building

─────────── **Thinking Time** ───────────

Read the next two questions. Answer them on the back of this paper.

1. In the third story, Willie eats a lot of sweets. Name foods that Willie should eat to be healthy.

2. Why was Ray unhappy about the change in the weather?

1. The main idea of this story is:
   a. changing weather
   b. a cloudy day
   c. an old umbrella

2. Anita liked:
   a. the sun
   b. the moon
   c. TV

3. Anita said she wanted to:
   a. be ready for the rain
   b. be ready for snow
   c. be ready for any kind of weather

4. Drenched means:
   a. very warm
   b. very cold
   c. very wet

5. You can tell that:
   a. The weatherman was right.
   b. The weatherman was wrong.
   c. The TV was broken.

6. The first thing Anita wore was:
   a. a raincoat and boots
   b. snowshoes and a jacket
   c. a sundress and sunglasses

★On the back of this paper, write about your favorite kind of weather and why you like it.

The Scary Movie

Name _____

1. **The main idea of this story is:**
   a. eating popcorn
   b. screaming in a movie
   c. enjoying a scary movie

2. **How did Hilda like the movie?**
   a. She didn't like it.
   b. She thought it was funny.
   c. She liked it a lot.

3. **The movie was called:**
   a. The Vampire Meets Godzilla
   b. The Vampire and the Bears
   c. Frankenstein and his Friends

4. **Risk means:**
   a. taking a bath
   b. taking a chance
   c. seeing a movie

5. **You can tell that:**
   a. No one was scared.
   b. Only Hilda was scared.
   c. Many people were scared.

6. **Before seeing the movie, Hilda:**
   a. ate her lunch
   b. read the newspaper
   c. called a friend

★On the back of this paper, write a paragraph about the kind of movie you like best. Why do you like it?

1. The main idea of this story is:
   a. a girl who can't see well
   b. a teacher who wears glasses
   c. kids who laugh

2. What couldn't Dolores do?
   a. jump rope
   b. read without glasses
   c. get a good math grade

3. Dolores couldn't see:
   a. the teacher
   b. herself
   c. the board

4. Punched out means:
   a. to drink punch
   b. to hit someone
   c. to step on a toe

5. You can guess the teacher:
   a. was glad about Dolores' glasses
   b. wore glasses, too
   c. told Dolores to go home

6. Dolores couldn't see well:
   a. before school
   b. before she got glasses
   c. after she wore her glasses

★On the back of this paper, write why you think Dolores was afraid that people would make fun of her.

Beware of Dog

1. The main idea of this story is:
a. a big dog
b. playing a trick
c. a mean cat

2. Lee and Don were ready:
a. to be bitten
b. to run away
c. to bite the dog

3. The name of Sondra's dog was:
a. Fireball
b. Tiger
c. Killer

4. <u>Beware</u> means:
a. be careful of something
b. wear something
c. carry something

5. Sondra probably thought her joke:
a. was silly
b. was mean
c. was funny

6. Before going to Sondra's:
a. Don ran into the house.
b. Don and Lee were afraid.
c. Killer bit Lee.

★On the back of this paper, write how Don and Lee could get even with Sondra.

Buried Treasure

Name _____

1. **The main idea of this story is:**
   a. a surprise treasure
   b. meeting pirates
   c. digging holes

2. **Willie followed a:**
   a. dog
   b. map
   c. leader

3. **Willie's dog was named:**
   a. Spotty
   b. Frisky
   c. Spotless

4. **A <u>treasure</u> is:**
   a. lots of junk
   b. buried bones
   c. something valuable

5. **You can guess that Spotless:**
   a. was happy to see his bones
   b. didn't care about his bones
   c. bit Willie on the hand

6. **Willie found the bones:**
   a. before he dug the hole
   b. after he dug the hole
   c. before he spoke to Spotless

★On the back of this paper, write what else Willie could have found.

FS-32018 Fourth Grade Activities

Messy Marvin

Name _____

1. **The main idea of this story is:**
   a. a fussy mother
   b. a sloppy boy
   c. a good night's sleep

2. **How did Marvin like his room?**
   a. He thought it was awful.
   b. It made his head hurt.
   c. He thought it was fine.

3. **Marvin found himself:**
   a. covered with toys and clothes
   b. out in a field
   c. sitting under a table

4. **To <u>disappear</u> is to:**
   a. come into a room
   b. pass out of sight
   c. suddenly be seen

5. **You can tell that:**
   a. Mom liked Marvin's room.
   b. The room was blue and green.
   c. Marvin's dream scared him.

6. **Before Marvin cleaned his room:**
   a. He fell asleep.
   b. He went for a walk.
   c. Mom washed his clothes.

★On the back of this paper, write why you think Marvin decided to keep his room clean.

1. The main idea of this story is:
   a. a lost kite
   b. a blue kite
   c. a torn kite

2. What was on the kite?
   a. Jenny's picture
   b. Jenny's address
   c. Kenny's phone number

3. The boy who sent the kite back:
   a. was from France
   b. was eight years old
   c. was from Japan

4. An <u>address</u> tells:
   a. where a place is found
   b. who lives in a house
   c. how many rooms are in a house

5. You can guess that:
   a. Jenny's kite was in a tree.
   b. Jenny's kite went very far.
   c. Jenny never got the letter.

6. After the kite went very high:
   a. The string broke.
   b. It fell on Jenny's house.
   c. Kenny found it.

★On the back of this paper, write an imaginary letter to Jenny's new friend in Japan.

1. **The main idea of this story is:**
   a. a sleepy dog
   b. a silly boy
   c. a smart dog

2. **How many tricks did Poopsie do?**
   a. one
   b. five
   c. three

3. **Guy asked Poopsie to:**
   a. roll over
   b. count to three
   c. speak

4. **A <u>genius</u> is:**
   a. very tall
   b. very smart
   c. beautiful

5. **Poopsie and Guy probably:**
   a. don't like each other
   b. have lots of fun
   c. are both dogs

6. **After Guy told him to roll over:**
   a. Poopsie rolled over.
   b. Poopsie didn't move.
   c. Poopsie barked.

★On the back of this paper, write a list of five tricks you'd like to teach a dog.

Reggie Robot

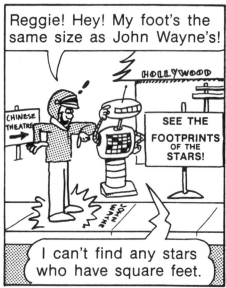

1. The main idea of this story is:
   a. getting in the movies
   b. a vacation trip
   c. a trip to Mars

2. Neptune and Pluto were:
   a. not close enough to home
   b. too big to visit
   c. too hot

3. Duke thinks that on Mars:
   a. People aren't nice.
   b. Those green guys talk too much.
   c. There are no people.

4. <u>Vacation</u> means:
   a. a place to eat
   b. a train trip
   c. a holiday

5. To what planet did they go?
   a. Venus
   b. Mercury
   c. Earth

6. The second place Reggie said was:
   a. Mars
   b. Mercury
   c. Pluto

★On the back of this paper, write about a great place on Earth that Reggie and Duke might like. Why would they like it?

 FS-32018 Fourth Grade Activities

Answer Key

Page 1

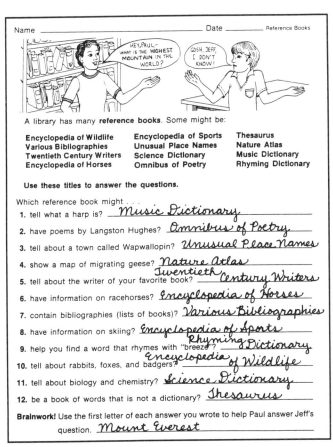

Name _____ Date _____ Reference Books

A library has many **reference books**. Some might be:

Encyclopedia of Wildlife	Encyclopedia of Sports	Thesaurus
Various Bibliographies	Unusual Place Names	Nature Atlas
Twentieth Century Writers	Science Dictionary	Music Dictionary
Encyclopedia of Horses	Omnibus of Poetry	Rhyming Dictionary

Use these titles to answer the questions.

Which reference book might . . .

1. tell what a harp is? *Music Dictionary*
2. have poems by Langston Hughes? *Omnibus of Poetry*
3. tell about a town called Wapwallopin? *Unusual Place Names*
4. show a map of migrating geese? *Nature Atlas*
5. tell about the writer of your favorite book? *Twentieth Century Writers*
6. have information on racehorses? *Encyclopedia of Horses*
7. contain bibliographies (lists of books)? *Various Bibliographies*
8. have information on skiing? *Encyclopedia of Sports*
9. help you find a word that rhymes with "breeze"? *Rhyming Dictionary*
10. tell about rabbits, foxes, and badgers? *Encyclopedia of Wildlife*
11. tell about biology and chemistry? *Science Dictionary*
12. be a book of words that is not a dictionary? *Thesaurus*

Brainwork! Use the first letter of each answer you wrote to help Paul answer Jeff's question. *Mount Everest*

Page 1

Page 2

Name _____ Date _____ Dictionary Specialties

Karen's dictionary had a Table of Contents. She found many things listed in the dictionary besides spelling and word meanings.

Karen looked at the **Tables of Measurement.** Now she could find how many ounces were in a pound, or how many feet in a mile. The **Metric Conversion Tables** told how to change miles to kilometers and pounds to kilograms. **Morse Code** told how to send messages in dot-dash. **Proofreaders' Symbols** helped Karen understand the marks her teacher put on her writing papers. Karen liked the Codes and Ciphers section best.

Here is a part of the Codes and Ciphers section.

CODE KEY
Use the code above to decipher this message.

You can find much
more in a dictionary
than just meanings
and spellings

Brainwork! Find a dictionary that has tables, codes and other information. List the titles of these information sections.

Page 2

Page 3

Name _____ Date _____ Dictionary Charts

Signs and Symbols -Astronomy	Music Symbols
● New Moon	♯ Sharp
☽ First Quarter Moon	♭ Flat
⊗ Full Moon	♮ Natural
⊕ ⊙ Earth	𝆯 Whole Note
☉ Sun	

Index of First Names and Their Meanings	
Alex, Alexander: leader of men	**David:** beloved
Alice, Allison: of noble rank	**Flora:** flower
Bob, Bobby, Rob, Robert: glory and bright	**George:** farmer
Carol, Caroline, Carolyn: feminine of Charles	**Harriet, Harriette:** fem. of Harry
Charles: man, warrior	**Harry, Henry:** home and kingdom

Susan's father's dictionary had a special section at the back that showed signs, symbols, and names. Some of the information Susan found is shown above. Use it to answer the questions.

1. Draw the symbol for the sun. ☉
2. Write the meaning of David. *beloved*
3. Show two symbols for the Full Moon. ○ ⊗
4. Draw the symbol for a musical sharp. ♯
5. What does Flora mean? *flower*
6. Draw three symbols for the earth. ⊕ ⊙ ⊖
7. Draw one symbol for the first quarter of the moon. *☽ or ◗*
8. What names mean the same as Robert? *Bob, Bobby, Rob*
9. What does Harriette mean? (Hint: see what Harry means.) *home and kingdom*

Brainwork! Look in a large dictionary to see what your name means. *answers will vary* . If your name is on this page, find out what the symbol © means. *copyright*

Page 3

Page 4

Name _____ Date _____ Publication Data

Henry's Horse
by
William Freitag
illustrated by
Dorothy Shepherd
Published by
Maris Gibson Co.
Dallas, Pennsylvania

Copyright 1981
William Freitag

All rights reserved.

Find and write in the correct answers.

The title page of Danny's library book tells us

1. the title of the book *Henry's Horse*
2. who wrote it (the author) *William Freitag*
3. who drew the pictures (the illustrator) *Dorothy Shepherd*
4. what company published the book *Maris Gibson Co.*
5. the city where it was published *Dallas, PA*

The back of the title page tells us the date when the book was copyrighted: *1981*

Danny noticed all his textbooks had a title page with the author's name, sometimes an illustrator, and the publisher's name and city. Some of the books had more than one author. *Answers will vary*

Brainwork! Look at the title pages of some of your textbooks. Write the titles, authors, publishers, city, and copyright dates on the chart below.

Subject	Title	Author(s)	Publisher	City	Date
Math					
Spelling					
Social Studies					
Science					

Page 4

FS-32018 Fourth Grade Activities

Answer Key

Page 5

Name _____ Date _____ Atlas Gazetteer

At the back of Kerry's atlas is a section called a **gazetteer**. A **gazetteer** is a geographical dictionary that lists all the places and geographical features in an atlas. Cities, states, rivers, and towns are listed alphabetically. A number in parentheses () after city, state, and county names gives the population. In **boldface** type after the page numbers are letters and numbers. These are called map coordinates. They help to locate a place on the map.

Here is a section of Kerry's **gazetteer**.

Columbia, Missouri (36,655)	page 56	**D 8**
Columbia, South Carolina (260,830)	page 71	**G 5**
Columbia Dam (Alabama)	page 34	**B 2**
Columbia Lake (British Columbia)	page 91	**A 7**
Columbia Mountains (Mexico)	page 99	**M 4**
Columbia River (U.S. and Canada)	page 92	**F 8**
Columbia Falls, Maine (442)	page 43	**A 1**

The map of Columbia, South Carolina, is on page _71_. Its population is _260,830_. Columbia Lake is in _British Columbia_. It is shown on the map on page _91_. Its coordinates are _A 7_. The Columbia _River_ is in the U.S. and Canada. Columbia Falls, Maine, has a population of _442_. The coordinates for Columbia dam are _B 2_. Which city named Columbia has the largest population? _Columbia, S.C._

Brainwork! Find your town or city in the **gazetteer** of an atlas. Write its population _____, the page _____, and coordinates _____

Page 5

Page 6

Name _____ Date _____ Cross References

George could not find the information he needed under <u>Sports</u> in his encyclopedia. At the end of the Sports article it said, "See also Baseball, Football, Soccer." George looked under the **cross reference**, Football, and found what he needed to know.

Use an encyclopedia to find what cross references are listed under the subjects below. If there are none, write "none." Write the name of the encyclopedia you used here. _Answers will vary_

1. Rattlesnakes _____
2. Hoover Dam _____
3. Mistletoe _____
4. Sahara _____
5. Henry VIII of England _____
6. Bogotá _____
7. Clarinet _____
8. Laser _____
9. Spiders _____
10. Broccoli _____

Brainwork! Look in the encyclopedia for <u>Michelangelo</u>. Write two paragraphs about this topic on the back of this paper.

Page 6

Page 7

Name _____ Date _____ Special Encyclopedias

Kimi found a shelf of special encyclopedias in the library. Each of these books was about only one general subject: music, birds, painting, others.

Write the name of the special subject encyclopedia to use on the line after each statement.

1. Mel's hobby is unusual wild animals. _Wildlife Encyclopedia_
2. Anne plays the clarinet. _Encyclopedia of Music_
3. Jamie wants to raise orchids. _Exotic Plant Encyclopedia_
4. Rob needs facts on soccer. _Encyclopedia of Sports and Games_
5. Melissa is a bird watcher. _Encyclopedia of American Birds_
6. Chris must report on a composer. _Encyclopedia of Music_
7. Bill wants to know about eagles. _Encyclopedia of American Birds_
8. Laurie is collecting coins. _Coin and Stamp Encyclopedia_
9. Sue wants to know about tennis. _Encyclopedia of Sports and Games_
10. Mike is interested in oil paintings. _Encyclopedia of Painting_

Brainwork! Make up a title for a special encyclopedia that would help you learn more about your own hobby, favorite sport, or other interest.
Answers will vary.

Page 7

Page 8

Name _____ Date _____ Title/Author Catalog

Jody's library has two card catalogs. One is labeled **Title/Author**. If Jody knows the title or author of a book she wants, she looks in that catalog. Jody looked at these cards.

Author Card

Title Card

751.422
Gal
Galvin, Ellen
Watercolor pa
Maris Gibson
115 p.

751.422
Gal
Watercolor Painting
Galvin, Ellen
Watercolor painting.
Maris Gibson Co, Dallas, Pa, 1981.
115 p. illus. photos plates

Jody wants to find the books below. If she should look for a title card, write title. If she should look for an author card, write author.

1. Little American _title_
2. James Scott _author_
3. My Friend Joe _title_
4. Johnny Onenote _author_
5. Paul Simpson _author_
6. Another Day _title_
7. Mary Bleck _author_
8. John L. Smith _author_
9. Your Horoscope _title_
10. Memories of Yesterday _title_
11. James M. Bradley _author_
12. Raising Orchids _title_

Underline the last name of each author above. Author cards are filed alphabetically according to last name.

Brainwork! What is the call number of the library book you are reading? _____ _Answers will vary_. If you do not have a library book, look for one in the library and write its call number.

Page 8

Answer Key

Kevin wanted to learn how to do watercolor painting. He looked in the library's **subject catalog** under Watercolor Painting. A card said, "See PAINTING." Kevin chose this card:

> 751.422 PAINTING
> Gal   Galvin, Ellen
>   Watercolor painting.
>   Maris Gibson Co., Dallas, PA, 1981.
>   115 p.   illus.   photos   plates
>   Illustrated step-by-step lessons in
>   beginning watercolor technique.
>
>   1. Painting   I. Author   II. Title

1. What is the call number of this book? _751.422 Gal_
2. Who wrote the book? _Ellen Galvin_
3. What is its title? _Watercolor Painting_
4. Who published the book? _Maris Gibson Co._
5. In what city was the book published? _Dallas, PA._
6. What is the copyright date of the book? _1981_
7. How is the book illustrated? _photos, plates_
8. Why do you think it might be a good book for beginners who want to learn about watercolor painting? _It says "beginning"_
9. Why would the book be less useful if it had no illustrations? _You need pictures to see how to do the paintings._
10. What is the subject under which the book is filed? _Painting_

Brainwork! Find three library books about Watercolor Painting. Write the titles.

Answers will vary

Page 9

Libraries put books on their shelves according to a special system. Most libraries use the **Dewey Decimal System**. In the Dewey Decimal System, books are put into categories or groups.

Books numbered:	are about:
000-099	general reference, encyclopedias
100-199	philosophy, thoughts, ideas
200-299	religion, myths
300-399	social science, folklore, fairy tales
400-499	languages, dictionaries
500-599	pure science: math, astronomy, botany, zoology, physics, chemistry, earth science
600-699	technology (useful sciences): medicine, engineering, home economics, agriculture
700-799	fine arts: music, art, drawing, sports, hobbies, photography
800-899	literature, plays, poetry
900-999	history, geography, travel

Write the Dewey Decimal category (Example: 500-599) after the titles below to show where these books would be shelved.

Grimm's Fairy Tales _300-399_   Dictionary of Language _400-499_
History of Europe _900-999_   Travel in Japan _900-999_
Photography _700-799_   Music for Strings _700-799_
Greek Myths _200-299_   Poetry, a Collection _800-899_
Philosophy of Mankind _100-199_   Medicine and Surgery _600-699_

Brainwork! Browse through the library shelves. Write the names of three books that have the call numbers between 600 and 699.

Answers will vary

Page 10

Unscramble the words to find out what Simon says.

Jason: Where should I look first for information for my science project?

Simon: Your niceecs book. _science_

Pam: I need to know. Where should I start?

Simon: Try your nauggeal book. _language_

Molly: Where can I find facts about the United States?

Simon: Your ilacssotiedus book, of course. _social studies_

When you need to know something about one of your school subjects such as math, science, social studies, language, or spelling, a good place to look first is in your textbook.

Write the kinds of textbooks you would use to find the following information.

1. measurement tables _math book_
2. punctuation _language book_
3. geographical terms _social studies book_
4. the order of the Solar System _science book_
5. rules for spelling the long e sound _spelling book_
6. correct form for a friendly letter _language book_
7. a list of U.S. presidents _social studies book_
8. metric measurement tables _math book_
9. maps of the world's rainfall _social studies book_
10. glossary of scientific terms _science book_

Brainwork! List three more kinds of information you can find in your math book.

answers will vary

Page 11

Larry asked the librarian to help him find information for his report on African elephants. She showed Larry magazines which had articles on elephants.

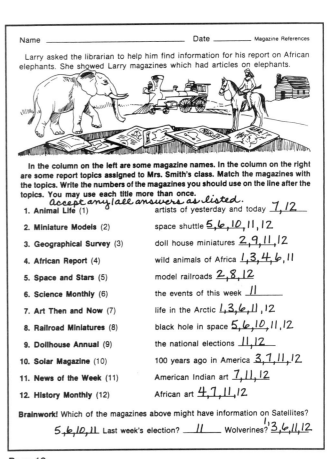

In the column on the left are some magazine names. In the column on the right are some report topics assigned to Mrs. Smith's class. Match the magazines with the topics. Write the numbers of the magazines you should use on the line after the topics. You may use each title more than once. _Accept any/all answers as listed._

1. Animal Life (1)   artists of yesterday and today _7, 12_
2. Miniature Models (2)   space shuttle _5, 6, 10, 11, 12_
3. Geographical Survey (3)   doll house miniatures _2, 9, 11, 12_
4. African Report (4)   wild animals of Africa _1, 3, 4, 6, 11_
5. Space and Stars (5)   model railroads _2, 8, 12_
6. Science Monthly (6)   the events of this week _11_
7. Art Then and Now (7)   life in the Arctic _1, 3, 6, 11, 12_
8. Railroad Miniatures (8)   black hole in space _5, 6, 10, 11, 12_
9. Dollhouse Annual (9)   the national elections _11, 12_
10. Solar Magazine (10)   100 years ago in America _3, 7, 11, 12_
11. News of the Week (11)   American Indian art _7, 11, 12_
12. History Monthly (12)   African art _4, 7, 11, 12_

Brainwork! Which of the magazines above might have information on Satellites?

_5, 6, 10, 11_ Last week's election? _11_ Wolverines? _1, 3, 6, 11, 12_

Page 12

Answer Key

Page 13

Tom read several articles in different magazines to get information for his report. His teacher asked him to list the articles he read at the end of his report. Tom wrote his Bibliography like this:

1) Author's last name, then first name. 2) title of the article. 3) name of magazine (underlined), 4) date of magazine.

Arrange the information below in the correct order with the correct punctuation.

a) News Monthly, June 1980, "Cattle Foods." Jane Galvin

b) Maria Mitchell, January 1887, "A New Comet." Science Monthly

c) October 1981, Science and Fiction, Brad Berry. "New Start."

d) "Cosmic Cosmos." January 1967, W.C. Are. Scientific Review

e) May 1978, "Atlantis Found." Exploration, Jan Jones

Author — (last name first)	Title of Article	Name of Magazine (underlined)	Date
Ex. Jones, Jan.	"Atlantis Found."	Exploration,	May 1978.
a. Galvin, Jane.	"Cattle Foods."	News Monthly,	June 1980.
b. Mitchell, Maria.	"A New Comet."	Science Monthly,	Jan. 1887.
c. Berry, Brad.	"New Stars."	Science and Fiction,	October 1981.
d. Are, W.C.	"Cosmic Cosmos."	Scientific Review,	Jan. 1967.

Brainwork! Find an article in a magazine that you can use in a report. Write down the author's name, the title of the article, the name of the magazine, and its date.

Answers will vary.

Page 13

Page 14

Joey always read the page in the newspaper that gave the complete weather report. He studied the weather maps and the pictures taken by satellite.

Here are some reports of the weather in several cities.

City	Lo/Hi	Precipitation	City	Lo/Hi	Precipitation
Albany	33/56	——	Juneau	43/49	1.61
Atlanta	59/83	——	Miami Beach	70/79	——
Boise	36/68	——	New York	44/66	——
Chicago	43/63	.17	Reno	26/70	——
Dallas	71/87	.03	St. Louis	62/69	1.10
Flagstaff	28/55	——	Spokane	31/61	——

1. Which city had the lowest low temperature? *Reno*
2. Where was the hottest high? *Dallas*
3. Where did it rain or snow (precip.)? *Chicago, Dallas, Juneau, St. Louis*
4. Which city had the most rain or snow? *Juneau*
5. Which cities had below-freezing (32°) lows? *Flagstaff, Reno, Spokane*
6. Which city had the greatest difference between low and high? *Reno*
   By how many degrees? *44°*
7. Which city had the least difference between high and low? *Juneau*
   By how many degrees? *6°*

Brainwork! Find the complete weather report in your paper. What city had the highest high? *answers vary* The lowest low? _____

Page 14

Page 15

The **classified** section of Terry's phone book (Yellow Pages) comes after the white pages. In some cities this is a separate book. Yellow Pages have advertisements as well as alphabetical listings within each **classification**. Some **classifications** are:

Automobile Body Repair
Automobile Dealers — New Cars
Automobile Dealers — Used Cars
Dog & Cat Doctors — See Veterinarians
Dog and Cat Grooming
Dolls
Florists — Retail
Florists — Wholesale
Hobby and Model Supplies
Judo, Karate, and Jujitsu
Kindergartens — See Nursery Schools
Moccasins — See Shoes, Retail

Modeling Schools
Motorcycles
Music Dealers — See Musical Instruments, Records, Phonograph, Stereophonic Equipment
Nurseries — Plants & Trees
Nursery Schools
Pizzas
Public Schools — See Schools, Elementary & Secondary
Skate Boards

If you want to call about . . . look under . . .

1. a sick dog — *Veterinarians*
2. model airplane kits — *Hobby and Model Supplies*
3. ordering a pizza — *Pizzas*
4. renting a clarinet — *Musical Instruments*
5. buying a rosebush — *Nurseries, Plants and Trees*
6. reporting sick at school — *Schools, Elementary & Secondary*
7. ordering flowers for Mom — *Florists, Retail*
8. kindergartens for sister Sue — *Nursery Schools*
9. repairing a dented fender — *Automobile Body Repair*
10. a bath and brushing for Fido — *Dog and Cat Grooming*
11. karate lessons — *Judo, Karate and Jujitsu*
12. a pair of moccasins — *Shoes, Retail*

Brainwork! Write the difference between **retail** and **wholesale**.

Page 15

Page 16

Mr. Quinn's **almanac** has almost 1000 pages of facts and information. Andrea found a table of distances like this:

	Albuquerque	Chicago	Denver	Los Angeles	New Orleans	Seattle
Albuquerque	——	1285	482	805	1145	1511
Chicago	1285	——	1018	2106	929	2013
Denver	482	1018	——	1162	1284	1377
Los Angeles	805	2106	1162	——	1916	1177
New Orleans	1145	929	1284	1916	——	2645
Seattle	1511	2013	1377	1177	2645	——

To find the distance from Los Angeles to Denver, find Los Angeles on the left side and Denver at the top. Run your finger across from Los Angeles and down from Denver. Where they meet you will find the distance, 1162 miles.

1. How far is it from Chicago to Seattle? *2013 miles*
2. What is the distance from Los Angeles to Chicago? *2106 miles*
3. How many miles from Albuquerque to New Orleans? *1145 miles*
4. Which two cities are closest together? *Albuquerque and Denver*
5. Which two cities are farthest apart? *New Orleans and Seattle*
6. Which is farther, Denver to New Orleans or Chicago to Albuquerque? *Chicago to Albuquerque*
7. Is Denver closer to Albuquerque or New Orleans? *Albuquerque*
8. Is Seattle closer to Denver or Los Angeles? *Los Angeles*

Brainwork! Find a table of distances in an almanac or other reference book. Find the distance from your city, or the nearest city to your home, to New York. _____ To San Francisco _____

To Miami _____

Page 16

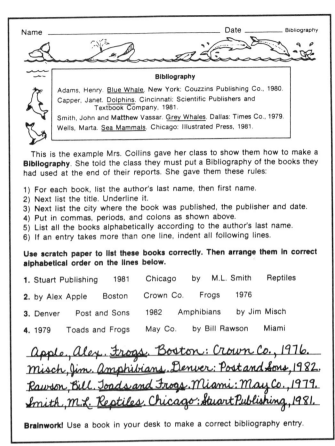

Name _____ **Date** _____ Bibliography

Bibliography

Adams, Henry. Blue Whale. New York: Couzzins Publishing Co., 1980.
Capper, Janet. Dolphins. Cincinnati: Scientific Publishers and
    Textbook Company, 1981.
Smith, John and Matthew Vassar. Grey Whales. Dallas: Times Co., 1979.
Wells, Marta. Sea Mammals. Chicago: Illustrated Press, 1981.

This is the example Mrs. Collins gave her class to show them how to make a **Bibliography**. She told the class they must put a Bibliography of the books they had used at the end of their reports. She gave them these rules:

1) For each book, list the author's last name, then first name.
2) Next list the title. Underline it.
3) Next list the city where the book was published, the publisher and date.
4) Put in commas, periods, and colons as shown above.
5) List all the books alphabetically according to the author's last name.
6) If an entry takes more than one line, indent all following lines.

Use scratch paper to list these books correctly. Then arrange them in correct alphabetical order on the lines below.

1. Stuart Publishing   1981   Chicago   by M.L. Smith   Reptiles

2. by Alex Apple   Boston   Crown Co.   Frogs   1976

3. Denver   Post and Sons   1982   Amphibians   by Jim Misch

4. 1979   Toads and Frogs   May Co.   by Bill Rawson   Miami

Apple, Alex. Frogs. Boston: Crown Co., 1976.
Misch, Jim. Amphibians. Denver: Post and Sons, 1982.
Rawson, Bill. Toads and Frogs. Miami: May Co., 1979.
Smith, M.L. Reptiles. Chicago: Stuart Publishing, 1981.

Brainwork! Use a book in your desk to make a correct bibliography entry.

Page 17

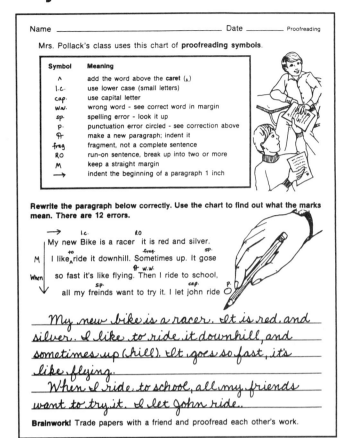

Name _____ **Date** _____ Proofreading

Mrs. Pollack's class uses this chart of **proofreading symbols**.

Symbol	Meaning
^	add the word above the caret (ʌ)
l.c.	use lower case (small letters)
cap.	use capital letter
w.w.	wrong word - see correct word in margin
sp.	spelling error - look it up
p.	punctuation error circled - see correction above
¶	make a new paragraph; indent it
frag	fragment, not a complete sentence
RO	run-on sentence, break up into two or more
M	keep a straight margin
→	indent the beginning of a paragraph 1 inch

Rewrite the paragraph below correctly. Use the chart to find out what the marks mean. There are 12 errors.

My new Bike is a racer it is red and silver.
I like ride it downhill. Sometimes up. It gose
so fast it's like flying. Then I ride to school,
all my freinds want to try it. I let john ride

My new bike is a racer. It is red and
silver. I like to ride it downhill, and
sometimes up (hill). It goes so fast, it's
like flying.
When I ride to school, all my friends
want to try it. I let John ride.

Brainwork! Trade papers with a friend and proofread each other's work.

Page 18

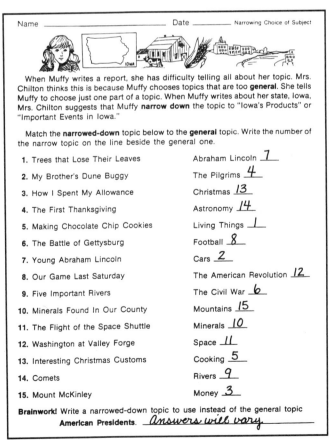

Name _____ **Date** _____ Narrowing Choice of Subject

When Muffy writes a report, she has difficulty telling all about her topic. Mrs. Chilton thinks this is because Muffy chooses topics that are too **general**. She tells Muffy to choose just one part of a topic. When Muffy writes about her state, Iowa, Mrs. Chilton suggests that Muffy **narrow down** the topic to "Iowa's Products" or "Important Events in Iowa."

Match the **narrowed-down** topic below to the **general** topic. Write the number of the narrow topic on the line beside the general one.

1. Trees that Lose Their Leaves	Abraham Lincoln ___7___
2. My Brother's Dune Buggy	The Pilgrims ___4___
3. How I Spent My Allowance	Christmas ___13___
4. The First Thanksgiving	Astronomy ___14___
5. Making Chocolate Chip Cookies	Living Things ___1___
6. The Battle of Gettysburg	Football ___8___
7. Young Abraham Lincoln	Cars ___2___
8. Our Game Last Saturday	The American Revolution ___12___
9. Five Important Rivers	The Civil War ___6___
10. Minerals Found In Our County	Mountains ___15___
11. The Flight of the Space Shuttle	Minerals ___10___
12. Washington at Valley Forge	Space ___11___
13. Interesting Christmas Customs	Cooking ___5___
14. Comets	Rivers ___9___
15. Mount McKinley	Money ___3___

Brainwork! Write a narrowed-down topic to use instead of the general topic **American Presidents.** *Answers will vary.*

Page 19

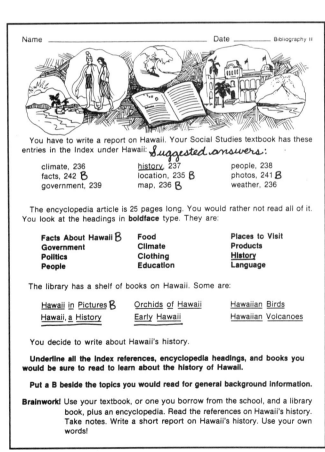

Name _____ **Date** _____ Bibliography II

You have to write a report on Hawaii. Your Social Studies textbook has these entries in the Index under Hawaii: *Suggested answers:*

climate, 236	history, 237	people, 238
facts, 242 B	location, 235 B	photos, 241 B
government, 239	map, 236 B	weather, 236

The encyclopedia article is 25 pages long. You would rather not read all of it. You look at the headings in **boldface** type. They are:

Facts About Hawaii B	Food	Places to Visit
Government	Climate	Products
Politics	Clothing	History
People	Education	Language

The library has a shelf of books on Hawaii. Some are:

Hawaii in Pictures B	Orchids of Hawaii	Hawaiian Birds
Hawaii, a History	Early Hawaii	Hawaiian Volcanoes

You decide to write about Hawaii's history.

Underline all the index references, encyclopedia headings, and books you would be sure to read to learn about the history of Hawaii.

Put a B beside the topics you would read for general background information.

Brainwork! Use your textbook, or one you borrow from the school, and a library book, plus an encyclopedia. Read the references on Hawaii's history. Take notes. Write a short report on Hawaii's history. Use your own words!

Page 20

Answer Key

Name _____   Skill: Following directions, Art

Box Art

Choose only one of the following—crayons, felt tip markers, colored pencils, or water colors. Then color the designs according to the steps below. *Answers vary*

☑ Color box 1 using all different colors.

☑ Select one color. Color box 2 using black, white and different shades (light to dark) of the selected color.

☑ Color box 3 using only warm colors (yellows, oranges, and reds). Color box 4 using only cool colors (greens, blues, and purples).

☑ Vincent Van Gogh was an artist who used long strokes or lines in much of his work. Color box 5 like box 1, but use lines instead of solid coloring to fill the spaces.

☑ Georges Seurat was an artist who used small dots and brush strokes to make the shapes and colors blend. Color box 6 like box 1, but use only dots to draw the design.

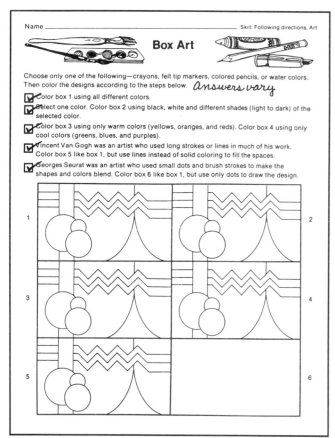

Page 21

Name _____

Directions:

☑ Write the letter above the soccer ball in box 1 below.
☑ Write the letter on the baseball in box 3.
☑ Write the letter on the soccer ball in box 6.
☑ Write the letter to the left of the baseball in box 8.
☑ Write the letter to the right of the football in box 4.
☑ Write the letter to the right of the soccer ball in box 10.
☑ Write the letter on the hockey stick in box 2.
☑ Write the letter above the football in box 5.
☑ Write the letter on the left side of the hockey stick in box 7.
☑ Write the letter on the football on box 9.

above ↑ | left ← → right | ↓ below

1	2	3	4		5	6	7	8	9	10
T	E	A	M		S	P	O	R	T	S

Page 22

Name _____

Directions: The ★ team and ● team are playing baseball. The ★ team is up to bat.

☑ Make ten ★s in the Star Dugout.
☑ Make five ●s in the Circle Dugout.
☑ Put a ● next to 1, 2 and 3.
☑ On the scoreboard write 2 for ● and 3 for ★.
☑ Draw a line to show the path of the ball from pitcher● to ★ at H;
   H to right field ●
   right field● back to pitcher●.
☑ Draw a dotted line----- to show path of ★ hitter from
   H to 1
   1 to 2
   2 to 3

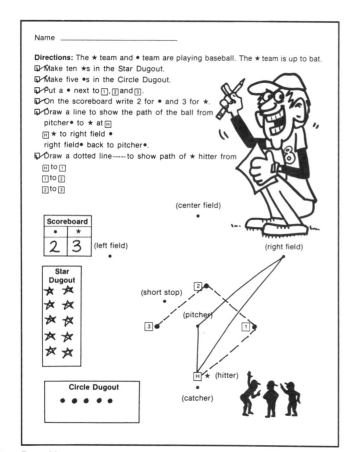

Page 23

Name _____

Directions: Mark each statement true or false by coloring the ○ . Then write the underlined letter in the blanks below. The number in ( ) tells you where to write the letter.

	True	False
☑ Dogs can laugh. (5)	○	●
☑ You can pick up a puppy. (3)	●	○
☑ You can't pick up an elephant. (12)	●	○
☑ Girls can be truck drivers. (6)	●	○
☑ All food must be cooked before eaten. (4)	○	●
☑ A feather is lighter than a book. (7)	●	○
☑ Children are younger than adults. (11)	●	○
☑ Hamburger is a vegetable. (1)	○	●
☑ A turtle's shell protects its soft body. (9)	●	○
☑ Apples are a kind of fruit. (8)	●	○
☑ Hot water can burn you. (2)	●	○
☑ Ice cubes are cold. (10)	●	○
☑ Young dogs are called kittens. (13)	○	●

To follow directions you must:

r	e	a	d		c	a	r	e	f	u	l	l	y
1	2	3	4		5	6	7	8	9	10	11	12	13

Page 24

Answer Key

111

Page 25

Name _____

You will get better grades if you

c o n c e n t r a t e on the directions!
1 2 3 4 5 6 7 8 9 10 11

Directions: Write letters on the lines above to find the missing word. Write the underlined letter on:

✓	line #1 of the word that comes first in the dictionary. <u>c</u>ube cup cuddle
✓	line #5 of the word that does not belong. apple ba<u>n</u>ana bed
✓	line #3 of the word that names the highest number. two ten thr<u>e</u>e
✓	line #11 of the word that names the lowest number. fifteen twenty fif<u>t</u>y
✓	line #9 of the word that names the tallest animal. lion giraff<u>e</u> monkey
✓	line #4 of the word that names the heaviest thing. feather book <u>c</u>ar
✓	line #7 of the thing that will float. <u>t</u>oothpick rock pin
✓	line #6 of the thing that will not float. <u>n</u>ail toothpick boat
✓	line #8 of the word that names the smallest animal. dog cat <u>r</u>at
✓	line #2 of the animal that makes no sound. c<u>a</u>t dog goldfish
✓	line #10 of the thing that is not alive. tree truck bird

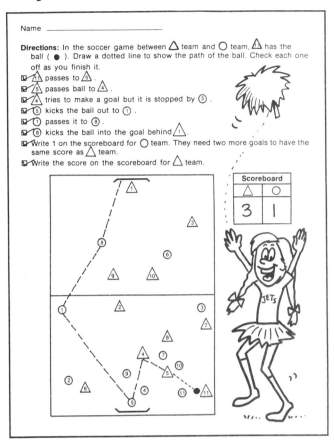

Page 26

Name _____

Directions: In the soccer game between △ team and ○ team, △ has the ball (●). Draw a dotted line to show the path of the ball. Check each one off as you finish it.

- ✓ △1 passes to △3 .
- ✓ △5 passes ball to △4 .
- ✓ △4 tries to make a goal but it is stopped by ○5 .
- ✓ ○5 kicks the ball out to ○1 .
- ✓ ○1 passes it to ○8 .
- ✓ ○8 kicks the ball into the goal behind △1 .
- ✓ Write 1 on the scoreboard for ○ team. They need two more goals to have the same score as △ team.
- ✓ Write the score on the scoreboard for △ team.

Scoreboard	
△	○
3	1

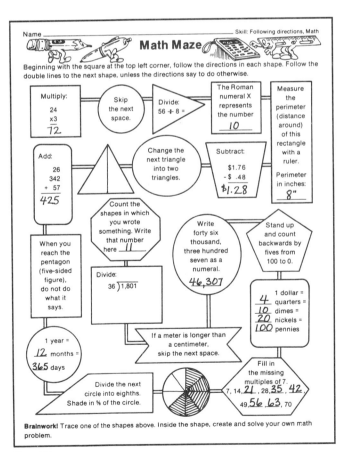

Page 27

Name _____   Skill: Following directions, Math

Math Maze

Beginning with the square at the top left corner, follow the directions in each shape. Follow the double lines to the next shape, unless the directions say to do otherwise.

Multiply:
24
×3
72

Skip the next space.

Divide:
56 ÷ 8 =

The Roman numeral X represents the number **10**

Measure the perimeter (distance around) of this rectangle with a ruler. Perimeter in inches: **8"**

Add:
26
342
+ 57
425

Change the next triangle into two triangles.

Subtract:
$1.76
- $ .48
$1.28

Count the shapes in which you wrote something. Write that number here **11**

Write forty six thousand, three hundred seven as a numeral. **46,307**

Stand up and count backwards by fives from 100 to 0.

When you reach the pentagon (five-sided figure), do not do what it says.

Divide:
36)1,801

1 dollar =
4 quarters =
10 dimes =
20 nickels =
100 pennies

1 year = **12** months = **365** days

If a meter is longer than a centimeter, skip the next space.

Fill in the missing multiples of 7. 7, 14, **21**, 28, **35**, **42**, 49, **56**, **63**, 70

Divide the next circle into eighths. Shade in ⅝ of the circle.

Brainwork! Trace one of the shapes above. Inside the shape, create and solve your own math problem.

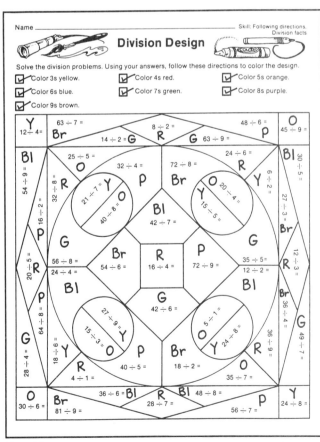

Page 28

Name _____   Skill: Following directions, Division facts

Division Design

Solve the division problems. Using your answers, follow these directions to color the design.

- ✓ Color 3s yellow.
- ✓ Color 4s red.
- ✓ Color 5s orange.
- ✓ Color 6s blue.
- ✓ Color 7s green.
- ✓ Color 8s purple.
- ✓ Color 9s brown.

Answer Key

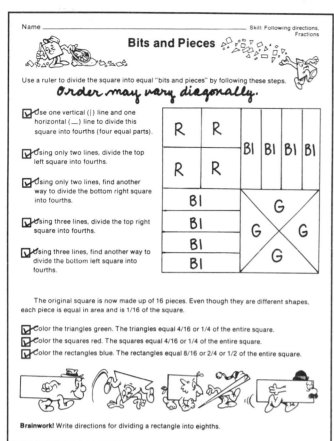

Bits and Pieces

Name _____ Skill: Following directions, Fractions

Use a ruler to divide the square into equal "bits and pieces" by following these steps.

Order may vary diagonally.

☑ Use one vertical (|) line and one horizontal (—) line to divide this square into fourths (four equal parts).

☑ Using only two lines, divide the top left square into fourths.

☑ Using only two lines, find another way to divide the bottom right square into fourths.

☑ Using three lines, divide the top right square into fourths.

☑ Using three lines, find another way to divide the bottom left square into fourths.

The original square is now made up of 16 pieces. Even though they are different shapes, each piece is equal in area and is 1/16 of the square.

☑ Color the triangles green. The triangles equal 4/16 or 1/4 of the entire square.

☑ Color the squares red. The squares equal 4/16 or 1/4 of the entire square.

☑ Color the rectangles blue. The rectangles equal 8/16 or 2/4 or 1/2 of the entire square.

Brainwork! Write directions for dividing a rectangle into eighths.

Page 29

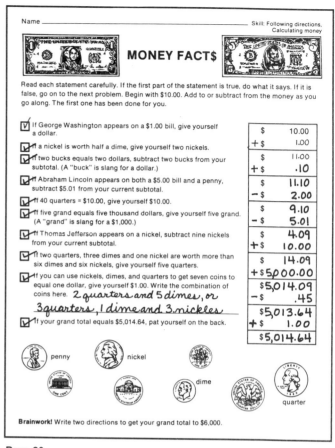

MONEY FACT$

Name _____ Skill: Following directions, Calculating money

Read each statement carefully. If the first part of the statement is true, do what it says. If it is false, go on to the next problem. Begin with $10.00. Add to or subtract from the money as you go along. The first one has been done for you.

☑ If George Washington appears on a $1.00 bill, give yourself a dollar.

☑ If a nickel is worth half a dime, give yourself two nickels.

☑ If two bucks equals two dollars, subtract two bucks from your subtotal. (A "buck" is slang for a dollar.)

☑ If Abraham Lincoln appears on both a $5.00 bill and a penny, subtract $5.01 from your current subtotal.

☑ If 40 quarters = $10.00, give yourself $10.00.

☑ If five grand equals five thousand dollars, give yourself five grand. (A "grand" is slang for a $1,000.)

☑ If Thomas Jefferson appears on a nickel, subtract nine nickels from your current subtotal.

☑ If two quarters, three dimes and one nickel are worth more than six dimes and six nickels, give yourself five quarters.

☑ If you can use nickels, dimes, and quarters to get seven coins to equal one dollar, give yourself $1.00. Write the combination of coins here. *2 quarters and 5 dimes, or 3 quarters, 1 dime and 3 nickles*

☑ If your grand total equals $5,014.64, pat yourself on the back.

$	10.00
+ $	1.00
$	11.00
+ $	.10
$	11.10
− $	2.00
$	9.10
− $	5.01
$	4.09
+ $	10.00
$	14.09
+ $	5,000.00
$	5,014.09
− $	.45
$	5,013.64
+ $	1.00
$	5,014.64

penny   nickel

dime   quarter

Brainwork! Write two directions to get your grand total to $6,000.

Page 30

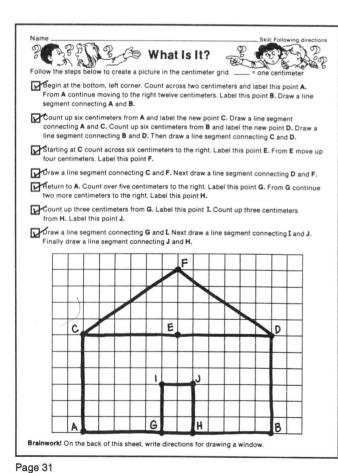

What Is It?

Name _____ Skill: Following directions

Follow the steps below to create a picture in the centimeter grid. □ = one centimeter

☑ Begin at the bottom, left corner. Count across two centimeters and label this point **A**. From **A** continue moving to the right twelve centimeters. Label this point **B**. Draw a line segment connecting **A** and **B**.

☑ Count up six centimeters from **A** and label the new point **C**. Draw a line segment connecting **A** and **C**. Count up six centimeters from **B** and label the new point **D**. Draw a line segment connecting **B** and **D**. Then draw a line segment connecting **C** and **D**.

☑ Starting at **C** count across six centimeters to the right. Label this point **E**. From **E** move up four centimeters. Label this point **F**.

☑ Draw a line segment connecting **C** and **F**. Next draw a line segment connecting **D** and **F**.

☑ Return to **A**. Count over five centimeters to the right. Label this point **G**. From **G** continue two more centimeters to the right. Label this point **H**.

☑ Count up three centimeters from **G**. Label this point **I**. Count up three centimeters from **H**. Label this point **J**.

☑ Draw a line segment connecting **G** and **I**. Next draw a line segment connecting **I** and **J**. Finally draw a line segment connecting **J** and **H**.

Brainwork! On the back of this sheet, write directions for drawing a window.

Page 31

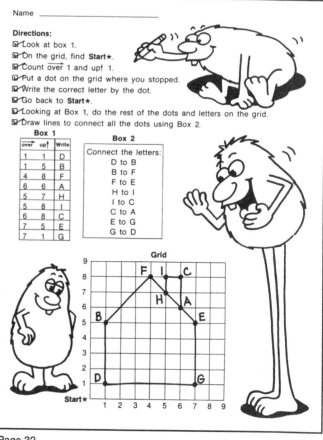

Name _____

Directions:

☑ Look at box 1.

☑ On the grid, find **Start★**.

☑ Count over 1 and up 1.

☑ Put a dot on the grid where you stopped.

☑ Write the correct letter by the dot.

☑ Go back to **Start★**.

☑ Looking at Box 1, do the rest of the dots and letters on the grid.

☑ Draw lines to connect all the dots using Box 2.

Box 1

over→	up↑	Write
1	1	D
1	5	B
4	8	F
5	7	H
5	8	I
6	8	C
7	5	E
7	1	G

Box 2

Connect the letters:
D to B
B to F
F to E
H to I
I to C
C to A
E to G
G to D

Grid

Page 32

Answer Key

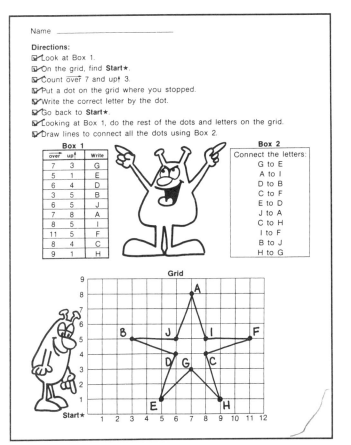

Page 33

Directions:
- ☑ Look at Box 1.
- ☑ On the grid, find **Start★**.
- ☑ Count over 7 and up 3.
- ☑ Put a dot on the grid where you stopped.
- ☑ Write the correct letter by the dot.
- ☑ Go back to **Start★**.
- ☑ Looking at Box 1, do the rest of the dots and letters on the grid.
- ☑ Draw lines to connect all the dots using Box 2.

Box 1

over	up	Write
7	3	G
5	1	E
6	4	D
3	5	B
6	5	J
7	8	A
8	5	I
11	5	F
8	4	C
9	1	H

Box 2

Connect the letters:
G to E
A to I
D to B
C to F
E to D
J to A
C to H
I to F
B to J
H to G

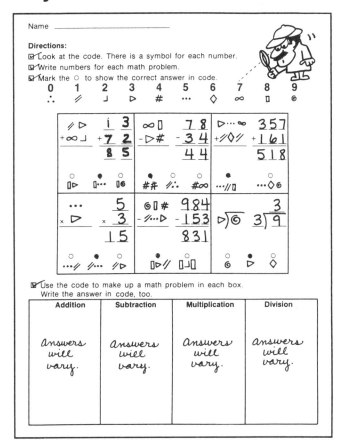

Page 34

Directions:
- ☑ Look at the code. There is a symbol for each number.
- ☑ Write numbers for each math problem.
- ☑ Mark the ○ to show the correct answer in code.

0	1	2	3	4	5	6	7	8	9
∴	⁄	⌐	▷	#	⋯	◇	∞	❒	⑥

☑ Use the code to make up a math problem in each box. Write the answer in code, too.

Addition	Subtraction	Multiplication	Division
answers will vary.	answers will vary.	answers will vary.	answers will vary.

Page 35

Directions: Put the answers on the Magic Math Square.

Z	E	J	S
5	13	6	2

D	Y	M	T
2	0	5	19

W	C	R	Q
6	11	5	4

V	K	I	G
13	2	10	1

Write the answer in

- ☑ 12 − 8 + 1 = **5** M
- ☑ 2 × **10** = 20 I
- ☑ 4 + 2 + 7 = **13** E
- ☑ 8 − 6 + **4** = 6 Q
- ☑ **2** × 9 = 18 K
- ☑ 100 − 99 = **1** G
- ☑ 20 − **5** = 15 Z
- ☑ 2 × 5 + 1 = **11** C
- ☑ 11 − 3 − 2 = **6** J
- ☑ 100 − 98 = **2** D
- ☑ 11 − 11 + 5 = **5** R
- ☑ 10 + 4 + 5 = **19** T

Magic Math Squares add up to the same total in each row going across or down.
- ☑ Figure out the "magic number".
- ☑ The "magic number" is **26**.
- ☑ Fill in the answers to the four empty squares.

Page 36

Directions: To find out the name of the state for each bird, write the letters on the correct lines as follows:
- ☑ Write the middle three letters of <u>stone</u> on lines 30, 31 and 32.
- ☑ On lines 4, 5, and 6 write the first three letters of <u>riddle</u>.
- ☑ On lines 24, 25 and 26 write the last three letters of <u>lash</u>.
- ☑ On line 17 write the middle letter in <u>nap</u>.
- ☑ Write the three middle letters in <u>paint</u> on lines 19, 20 and 21.
- ☑ On lines 11 and 12 write the middle two letters of <u>lift</u>.
- ☑ Write the first letter in <u>eye</u> on line 22.
- ☑ On lines 13, 14 and 15 write the last three letters of <u>corn</u>.
- ☑ On line 18 write the first letter of <u>mother</u>.
- ☑ On line 23 write the last letter of <u>cow</u>.
- ☑ Write the middle three letters of <u>scalp</u> on lines 8, 9 and 10.
- ☑ On lines 27, 28 and 29 write the last three letters of <u>talking</u>.
- ☑ On line 7 write the middle letter of <u>rag</u>.
- ☑ Write the first letter of <u>inside</u> on line 16.
- ☑ On lines 1, 2 and 3 write the three beginning letters of <u>float</u>.
- ☑ Capitalize the first letter of each state.

State Birds

Mockingbird — Florida
Quail — California
Chickadee — Maine
Willow Goldfinch — Washington

Answer Key

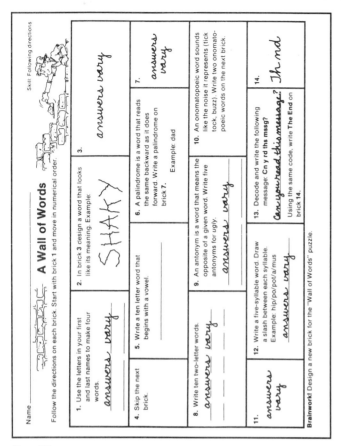

Page 37

Skill: Following directions

Name _____

A Wall of Words

Follow the directions on each brick. Start with brick 1 and move in numerical order.

1. Use the letters in your first and last names to make four words. *answers vary*
2. In brick 3 design a word that looks like its meaning. Example: *SHAKY*
3. *answers vary*
4. Skip the next brick.
5. Write a ten letter word that begins with a vowel.
6. A palindrome is a word that reads the same backward as it does forward. Write a palindrome on brick 7. Example: dad
7. *answers vary*
8. Write ten two-letter words. *answers vary*
9. An antonym is a word that means the opposite of a given word. Write five antonyms for *ugly*. *answers vary*
10. An onomatopoeic word sounds like the noise it represents (tick tock, buzz). Write two onomatopoeic words on the next brick.
11. *answers vary*
12. Write a five-syllable word. Draw a slash between each syllable. Example: hip/po/pot/a/mus *answers vary*
13. Decode and write the following message: **Cn y rd ths mssg?** Can you read this message?
14. Using the same code, write **The End** on brick 14. *Th nd*

Brainwork! Design a new brick for the "Wall of Words" puzzle.

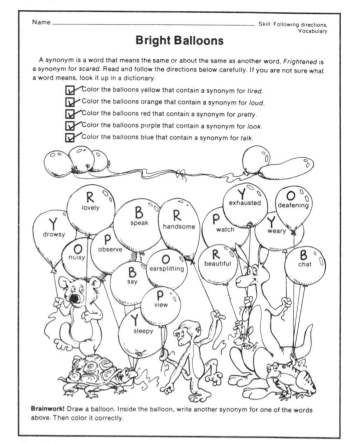

Page 38

Name _____ Skill: Following directions, Vocabulary

Bright Balloons

A synonym is a word that means the same or about the same as another word. *Frightened* is a synonym for *scared*. Read and follow the directions below carefully. If you are not sure what a word means, look it up in a dictionary.

- ☑ Color the balloons yellow that contain a synonym for *tired*.
- ☑ Color the balloons orange that contain a synonym for *loud*.
- ☑ Color the balloons red that contain a synonym for *pretty*.
- ☑ Color the balloons purple that contain a synonym for *look*.
- ☑ Color the balloons blue that contain a synonym for *talk*.

Balloons: lovely (R), drowsy (Y), noisy (O), speak (B), observe (P), say (B), earsplitting (O), view (P), sleepy (Y), handsome (R), watch (P), beautiful (R), weary (Y), exhausted (Y), deafening (O), chat (B)

Brainwork! Draw a balloon. Inside the balloon, write another synonym for one of the words above. Then color it correctly.

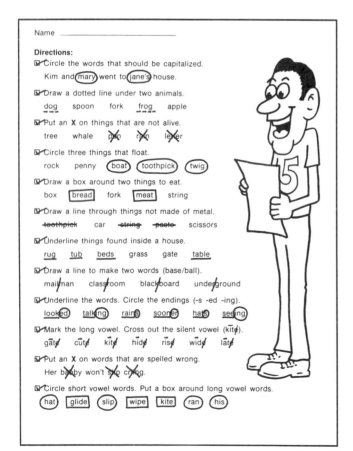

Page 39

Name _____

Directions:

- ☑ Circle the words that should be capitalized.
  Kim and (mary) went to (jane's) house.
- ☑ Draw a dotted line under two animals.
  <u>dog</u> spoon fork <u>frog</u> apple
- ☑ Put an **X** on things that are not alive.
  tree whale pen(X) ran(X) letter(X)
- ☑ Circle three things that float.
  rock penny (boat) (toothpick) (twig)
- ☑ Draw a box around two things to eat.
  box [bread] fork [meat] string
- ☑ Draw a line through things not made of metal.
  ~~toothpick~~ car ~~string~~ ~~paste~~ scissors
- ☑ Underline things found inside a house.
  <u>rug</u> <u>tub</u> <u>beds</u> grass gate <u>table</u>
- ☑ Draw a line to make two words (base/ball).
  mail/man class/room black/board under/ground
- ☑ Underline the words. Circle the endings (-s -ed -ing).
  <u>look</u>(ed) <u>talk</u>(ing) <u>rain</u>(s) <u>soon</u>(er) <u>hat</u>(s) <u>see</u>(ing)
- ☑ Mark the long vowel. Cross out the silent vowel (kite).
  gate cute kite hide rise wide late
- ☑ Put an **X** on words that are spelled wrong.
  Her baby won't stop crying.
- ☑ Circle short vowel words. Put a box around long vowel words.
  (hat) [glide] (slip) [wipe] [kite] (ran) (his)

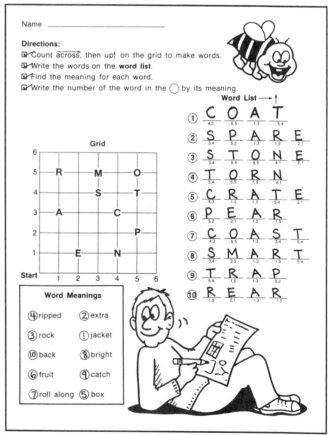

Page 40

Name _____

Directions:

- ☑ Count <u>across</u>, then up↑ on the grid to make words.
- ☑ Write the words on the **word list**.
- ☑ Find the meaning for each word.
- ☑ Write the number of the word in the ◯ by its meaning.

Grid

	1	2	3	4	5	6
6						
5	R		M		O	
4			S		T	
3	A			C		
2				P		
1		E		N		

Start

Word List →↑

1. C O A T (4,3 5,5 1,3 5,4)
2. S P A R E (3,4 5,2 1,3 5,5 2,1)
3. S T O N E (3,4 5,4 5,5 4,1 2,1)
4. T O R N (5,4 5,5 5,5 4,1)
5. C R A T E (4,3 5,5 1,3 5,4 2,1)
6. P E A R (5,2 2,1 1,3 5,5)
7. C O A S T (4,3 5,5 1,3 3,4 5,4)
8. S M A R T (3,4 3,5 1,3 5,5 5,4)
9. T R A P (5,4 5,5 1,3 5,2)
10. R E A R (1,5 2,1 1,3 5,5)

Word Meanings

- ④ ripped
- ② extra
- ③ rock
- ① jacket
- ⑩ back
- ⑧ bright
- ⑥ fruit
- ⑨ catch
- ⑦ roll along
- ⑤ box

Answer Key

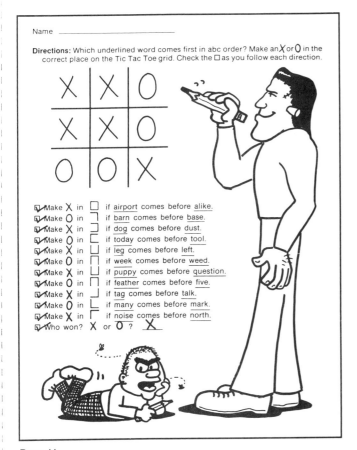

Name _____

Directions: Which underlined word comes first in abc order? Make an X or O in the correct place on the Tic Tac Toe grid. Check the □ as you follow each direction.

X	X	O
X	X	O
O	O	X

- ☑ Make X in □ if airport comes before alike.
- ☑ Make O in □ if barn comes before base.
- ☑ Make X in □ if dog comes before dust.
- ☑ Make O in □ if today comes before tool.
- ☑ Make X in □ if leg comes before left.
- ☑ Make O in □ if week comes before weed.
- ☑ Make X in □ if puppy comes before question.
- ☑ Make O in □ if feather comes before five.
- ☑ Make X in □ if tag comes before talk.
- ☑ Make O in □ if many comes before mark.
- ☑ Make X in □ if noise comes before north.
- ☑ Who won? X or O ? X

Page 41

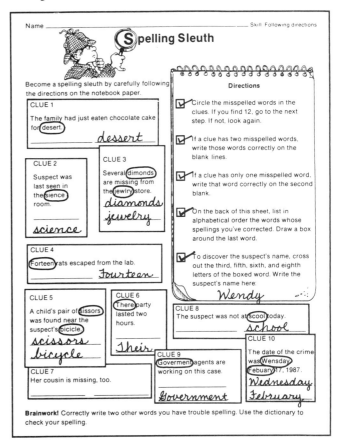

Name _____   Skill: Following directions

Spelling Sleuth

Become a spelling sleuth by carefully following the directions on the notebook paper.

Directions
- ☑ Circle the misspelled words in the clues. If you find 12, go to the next step. If not, look again.
- ☑ If a clue has two misspelled words, write those words correctly on the blank lines.
- ☑ If a clue has only one misspelled word, write that word correctly on the second blank.
- ☑ On the back of this sheet, list in alphabetical order the words whose spellings you've corrected. Draw a box around the last word.
- ☑ To discover the suspect's name, cross out the third, fifth, sixth, and eighth letters of the boxed word. Write the suspect's name here: Wendy

CLUE 1
The family had just eaten chocolate cake for desert.
dessert

CLUE 2
Suspect was last seen in the sience room.
science

CLUE 3
Several dimonds are missing from the jewlry store.
diamonds
jewelry

CLUE 4
Forteen rats escaped from the lab.
Fourteen

CLUE 5
A child's pair of sissors was found near the suspect's bicicle.
scissors
bicycle

CLUE 6
There party lasted two hours.
Their

CLUE 7
Her cousin is missing, too.

CLUE 8
The suspect was not at scool today.
school

CLUE 9
Goverment agents are working on this case.
Government

CLUE 10
The date of the crime was Wensday Febuary 17, 1987.
Wednesday
February

Brainwork! Correctly write two other words you have trouble spelling. Use the dictionary to check your spelling.

Page 42

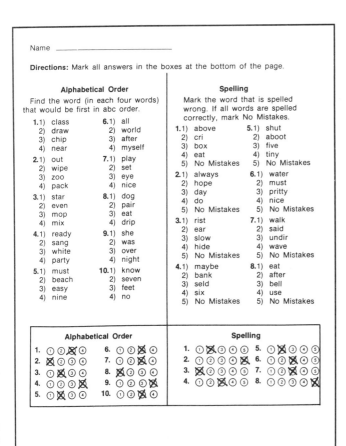

Name _____

Directions: Mark all answers in the boxes at the bottom of the page.

Alphabetical Order
Find the word (in each four words) that would be first in abc order.

1. 1) class
   2) draw
   3) chip
   4) near

2. 1) out
   2) wipe
   3) zoo
   4) pack

3. 1) star
   2) even
   3) mop
   4) mix

4. 1) ready
   2) sang
   3) white
   4) party

5. 1) must
   2) beach
   3) easy
   4) nine

6. 1) all
   2) world
   3) after
   4) myself

7. 1) play
   2) set
   3) eye
   4) nice

8. 1) dog
   2) pair
   3) eat
   4) drip

9. 1) she
   2) was
   3) over
   4) night

10. 1) know
    2) seven
    3) feet
    4) no

Spelling
Mark the word that is spelled wrong. If all words are spelled correctly, mark No Mistakes.

1. 1) above
   2) cri
   3) box
   4) eat
   5) No Mistakes

2. 1) always
   2) hope
   3) day
   4) do
   5) No Mistakes

3. 1) rist
   2) ear
   3) slow
   4) hide
   5) No Mistakes

4. 1) maybe
   2) bank
   3) seld
   4) six
   5) No Mistakes

5. 1) shut
   2) aboot
   3) five
   4) tiny
   5) No Mistakes

6. 1) water
   2) must
   3) pritty
   4) nice
   5) No Mistakes

7. 1) walk
   2) said
   3) undir
   4) wave
   5) No Mistakes

8. 1) eat
   2) after
   3) bell
   4) use
   5) No Mistakes

Alphabetical Order
1. ①②🅇④
2. 🅇②③④
3. ①🅇③④
4. ①②🅇④
5. ①🅇③④
6. ①②🅇④
7. ①②③🅇
8. 🅇②③④
9. ①②🅇④
10. ①②🅇④

Spelling
1. ①🅇③④⑤
2. ①②③④🅇
3. 🅇②③④⑤
4. ①🅇③④⑤
5. ①🅇③④⑤
6. ①②③④🅇
7. ①②🅇④⑤
8. ①②③④🅇

Page 43

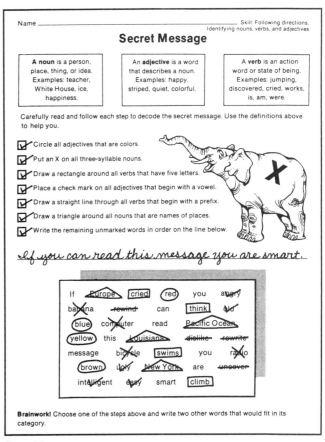

Name _____   Skill: Following directions, Identifying nouns, verbs, and adjectives

Secret Message

| **A noun** is a person, place, thing, or idea. Examples: teacher, White House, ice, happiness. | An **adjective** is a word that describes a noun. Examples: happy, striped, quiet, colorful. | A **verb** is an action word or state of being. Examples: jumping, discovered, cried, works, is, am, were. |

Carefully read and follow each step to decode the secret message. Use the definitions above to help you.

- ☑ Circle all adjectives that are colors.
- ☑ Put an X on all three-syllable nouns.
- ☑ Draw a rectangle around all verbs that have five letters.
- ☑ Place a check mark on all adjectives that begin with a vowel.
- ☑ Draw a straight line through all verbs that begin with a prefix.
- ☑ Draw a triangle around all nouns that are names of places.
- ☑ Write the remaining unmarked words in order on the line below.

If you can read this message you are smart.

If	Europe	cried	red	you	angry
banana	rewind	can	think	old
blue	computer	read	Pacific Ocean
yellow	this	Louisiana	dislike	rewrite
message	bicycle	swims	you	radio
brown	ugly	New York	are	uncover
intelligent	easy	smart	climb

Brainwork! Choose one of the steps above and write two other words that would fit in its category.

Page 44

---

115   FS-32018 Fourth Grade Activities

Answer Key

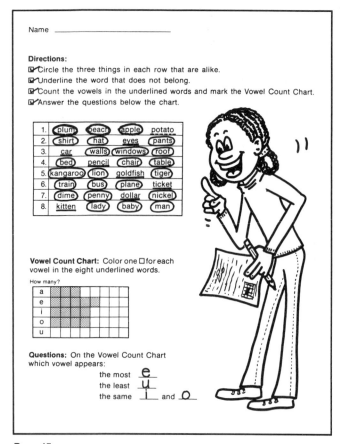

Page 45

Name _____

Directions:
☑ Circle the three things in each row that are alike.
☑ Underline the word that does not belong.
☑ Count the vowels in the underlined words and mark the Vowel Count Chart.
☑ Answer the questions below the chart.

1.	(plum)	(peach)	(apple)	potato
2.	(shirt)	(hat)	eyes	(pants)
3.	car	(walls)	(windows)	(roof)
4.	(bed)	pencil	(chair)	(table)
5.	kangaroo	(lion)	goldfish	(tiger)
6.	(train)	(bus)	(plane)	ticket
7.	(dime)	(penny)	dollar	(nickel)
8.	kitten	(lady)	(baby)	(man)

Vowel Count Chart: Color one ☐ for each vowel in the eight underlined words.

How many?

a					
e					
i					
o					
u					

Questions: On the Vowel Count Chart which vowel appears:

the most _e_
the least _u_
the same _i_ and _o_

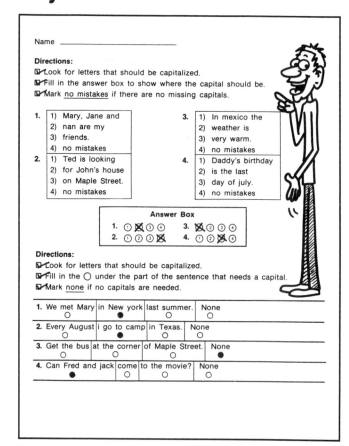

Page 46

Name _____

Directions:
☑ Look for letters that should be capitalized.
☑ Fill in the answer box to show where the capital should be.
☑ Mark no mistakes if there are no missing capitals.

1.
1) Mary, Jane and
2) nan are my
3) friends.
4) no mistakes

3.
1) In mexico the
2) weather is
3) very warm.
4) no mistakes

2.
1) Ted is looking
2) for John's house
3) on Maple Street.
4) no mistakes

4.
1) Daddy's birthday
2) is the last
3) day of july.
4) no mistakes

Answer Box
1. ① ⊗ ③ ④   3. ⊗ ② ③ ④
2. ① ② ⊗ ④   4. ① ② ⊗ ④

Directions:
☑ Look for letters that should be capitalized.
☑ Fill in the ○ under the part of the sentence that needs a capital.
☑ Mark none if no capitals are needed.

1. We met Mary	in New york	last summer.	None
○	●	○	○
2. Every August	i go to camp	in Texas.	None
○	●	○	○
3. Get the bus	at the corner	of Maple Street.	None
○	○	○	●
4. Can Fred and jack	come	to the movie?	None
●	○	○	○

Page 47

Name _____

Directions:
☑ Use words in the word box. ✔ each word as you use it.
☑ Write synonyms (words with about the same meaning) across.
☑ Write antonyms (words with opposite meanings) down.
☑ Draw ▨ in the unused squares on the puzzle to fill them in.

1. antonym for below
2. means the same as gift
3. synonym for huge
4. antonym for win
5. antonym for heavy
6. means the same as happy
7. synonym for sick
8. opposite of day
9. synonym for fast
10. opposite of far

Word Box
✔ present   ✔ cheerful
✔ light   ✔ night
✔ ill   ✔ lose
✔ quick   ✔ above
✔ enormous   ✔ close

q u i c k
l o
o s
n o r m o u s
i e
g
c h e e r f u l
t i
l g
o h
s t
p r e s e n t
e

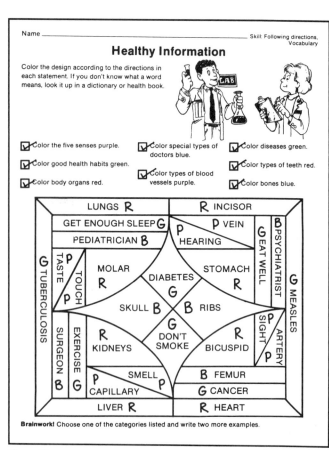

Page 48

Name _____   Skill: Following directions, Vocabulary

Healthy Information

Color the design according to the directions in each statement. If you don't know what a word means, look it up in a dictionary or health book.

☑ Color the five senses purple.
☑ Color good health habits green.
☑ Color body organs red.

☑ Color special types of doctors blue.
☑ Color types of blood vessels purple.

☑ Color diseases green.
☑ Color types of teeth red.
☑ Color bones blue.

LUNGS R | R INCISOR
GET ENOUGH SLEEP G | P VEIN
PEDIATRICIAN B | HEARING
TUBERCULOSIS G | TASTE P | TOUCH P | MOLAR R | DIABETES G | STOMACH R | EAT WELL B | PSYCHIATRIST G | MEASLES
SKULL B | B RIBS
SURGEON B | EXERCISE G | KIDNEYS R | DON'T SMOKE G | BICUSPID R | SIGHT P | ARTERY
SMELL P | P CAPILLARY | B FEMUR
LIVER R | G CANCER
R HEART

Brainwork! Choose one of the categories listed and write two more examples.

Answer Key

Page 49

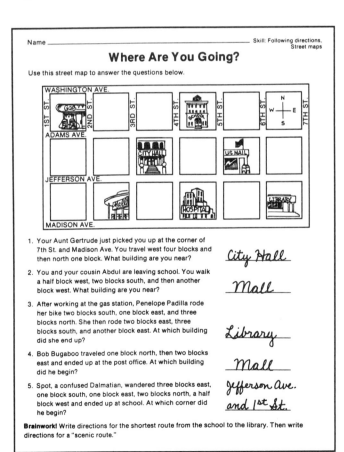

Page 51

Amazing Animals

Canis rufus is the scientific name for an endangered animal that lives in the United States. Read the statements about animals. Follow the directions only if the first part of the statement is correct. When you finish, you will know the common name of the *canis rufus*. If you are unsure of a word, look it up in a dictionary.

R E D   W O L F
1 2 3   4 5 6 7

☑ If a dromedary is a camel with three humps, place a B on space 4.
☑ If a tarantula is a hairy spider, place an L on space 6.
☑ If the elephant is the largest land animal, place an R on space 1.
☑ If a female horse is called a mare, skip the next statement.
☑ If a baby kangaroo travels in its mother's pouch, place a T on space 4.
☑ If humans are the fastest animals on land, place a P on space 4.
☑ If a boar is a wild pig, place an F on space 7.
☑ If the blue whale is the largest animal, place an O on space 5.
☑ If a weasel is smaller than a cow, place a D on space 3.
☑ If an opossum is a type of bird, place a Y on space 7.
☑ If a caterpillar changes into a moth or butterfly, place a W on space 4.
☑ If an owl is the largest bird, place an R on space 5.
☑ If a crocodile and an alligator are exactly the same, place an A on space 2.
☑ If a group of lions is called a pride, place an E on space 2.

Brainwork! On the back of this sheet, write three animal facts.

Page 50

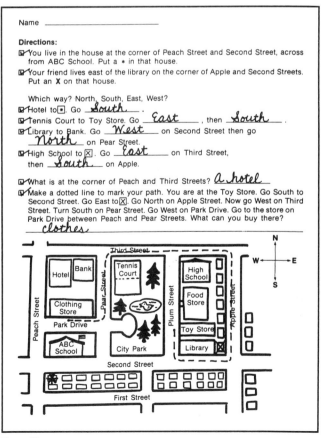

Page 52

Answer Key

Page 53

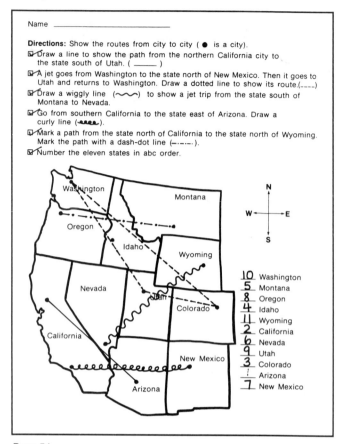

Page 54

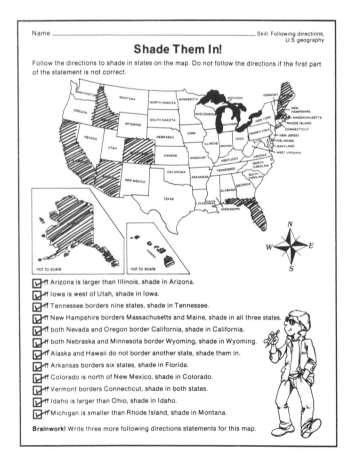

Page 55

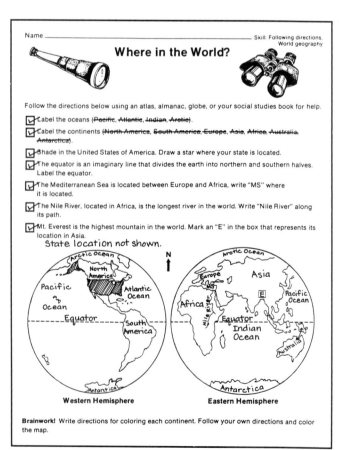

Page 56

Answer Key

© Frank Schaffer Publications, Inc.

119

FS-32018 Fourth Grade Activities

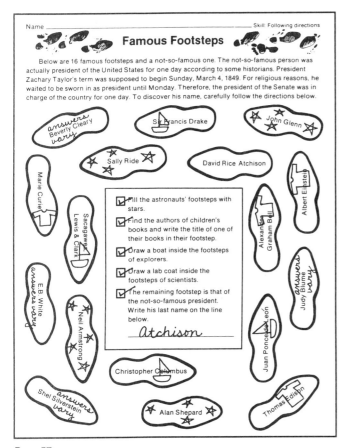

Page 57

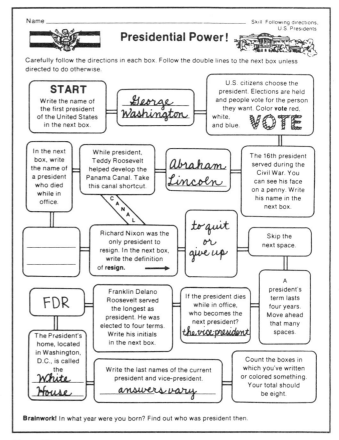

Page 58

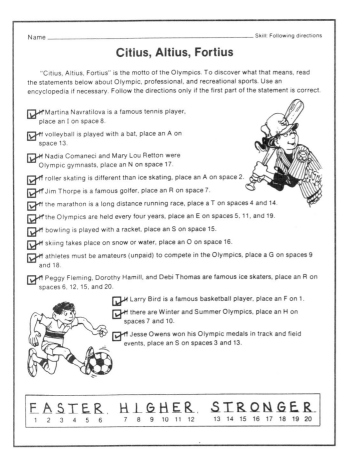

Page 59

Guide Time

Guide words are listed at the top of each dictionary page. They tell us the first and last words we will find on that page.

Find each of the words listed below in your dictionary. Next to each word, write the guide words on the page where you found the word.

1. decrease _Answers vary with dictionary used._
2. frame
3. hearth
4. incident
5. merchant
6. needle
7. otter
8. preview
9. salvage
10. symptom
11. trade
12. vessel

Page 60

Answer Key

More Guide Words

Use your dictionary to find each word listed below. Write the guide words you find on the same page. Next, write the entry word that comes just before the word you are looking for.

EXAMPLE: entry word to find | guide words | entry word before
late | larder-lath | latch string

	GUIDE WORDS	ENTRY WORD BEFORE
1. fish	*Answers vary with dictionary used.*	
2. collide		
3. betray		
4. intersect		
5. lecture		
6. mimic		
7. partridge		
8. policy		
9. tag		
10. tablet		
11. shirk		
12. remnant		

Celebrity Sweepstakes

Put yourself in the dictionary. Write 5 words that would come before your name, and five that would follow it. Don't forget you need to use your last name.

EXAMPLE:
1. leg
2. letter
3. lily
4. lime
5. limit
Lincoln, Abraham
1. line
2. linear
3. link
4. linkage
5. lint

YOUR LIST
1. ____
2. *answers vary*
3. ____
4. ____
5. ____

1. ____
2. ____
3. ____
4. ____
5. ____

Now put a friend or your teacher in the dictionary the same way.
1. *Answers vary*
2. ____
3. ____
4. ____
5. ____

I'll do Wilma.

1. ____
2. ____
3. ____
4. ____
5. ____

Answers vary with dictionary used.

Repeat

The dictionary respells words to help you pronounce the ones you don't know. Find each word below in the dictionary. Write the respelling. Be sure to leave space between the syllables and show the accent marks.

EXAMPLE: balloon (bə lün')

1. loaf ___lōf___
2. illegal ___i lē' gal___
3. extend ___eks 'tend'___
4. design ___di zīn'___
5. desire ___di zīr'___
6. caret ___kar' it___
7. caribou ___kar' ə boo___
8. bewitch ___bi wich'___
9. appeal ___ə pēl'___
10. better ___bet' ər___

Guess which one I am!

Now, rewrite the paragraph below. Replace the respelling with the real word it stands for.

Baseball is my (fā'vər it) game. I (prak'tis) whenever I have a (spar) (min'it). I (hōp) that someday I'll be a (fā məs) (stär). Dad (sed) he would get me a (nū) (gluv) for my (bérth' dā). I can hardly (wāt) for that (dā).

Baseball is my favorite game. I practice whenever I have a spare minute. I hope that someday I'll be a famous star. Dad said he would get me a new glove for my birthday. I can hardly wait for that day.

Answers vary with dictionary used

Play That One Again

Use your dictionary to help you rewrite each word below showing its pronunciation. Don't forget to mark those vowels where needed. Next to each word, write the number of syllables you have shown in the word.

EXAMPLE: beat · bēt 1

1. nonsense ___non' sens___ 2
2. induction ___in duk' shan___ 3
3. formless* ___fôrm' lis___ 2
4. crow ___krō___ 1
5. cucumber ___kū' kum bər___ 3
6. fellow ___fəl' ō___ 2
7. harvest ___här vist___ 2
8. interstate ___in'tər stāt___ 3
9. medicated ___med' ə kāt id___ 4
10. meaty ___mēt'i___ 2
11. react ___ri akt'___ 2
12. rowdy ___rou' di___ 2

One, two...

*Use the word formless in a sentence. (be sure to check its meaning.)

___*Answers vary.*___

What does the suffix less mean in the word formless?

___*without*___

Answer Key

Name _____ Skill: Meanings

Game Words

Write one game each of these things might be used in.
Use each word in a sentence.

EXAMPLE: puck   hockey   We used a puck in our hockey game.

Probable answers: *Sentences will vary.*

1. set *tennis*
2. wicket *cricket*
3. iron *golf*
4. touchdown *football*
5. goalie *soccer, hockey, or water polo*
6. infield *baseball*
7. field goal *football*
8. trump *bridge*
9. Ace *any card game*
10. balk *baseball*
11. quiver *archery*
12. basket *basketball*
13. down *football*
14. love *tennis*

I'm ready!

Page 65

Name _____ Skill: Multiple Pronunciation

What's What

Some words may be pronounced more than one way. Look for each of these words and write both respellings.

EXAMPLE: rodeo   rō′dē ō   or   rō dā′ō

1. catsup *kech′ əp or kat′ səp*
2. cerebral *ser′ ə brəl or sə rē′ brəl*
3. detail *di tāl′ or dē′ tāl*
4. consort *kän′ sôrt or kən sôrt*
5. contrite *kən trīt′ or kän′ trīt*
6. cooperative *kō äp′ ər ə tiv or cō op′ ar a tiv*
7. bouquet *bū kā′ or bō kā′*
8. adult *a dult′ or ad′ ult*
9. syrup *sir′ əp or ser′ əp*
10. substitute *sub′ stə tüt or sub′ sta tūt*

Now, try to pronounce each word in the two ways you have shown. Put a circle around the respelling that shows the way you say the word, or have heard it said most often.

It's rō′dē ō!   I say rō dā′ō!

Page 66

Name _____ Skill: Abbreviations

Short Stuff

Dictionaries help us spell and understand abbreviations. Find each abbreviation in your dictionary. Write the meaning.

1. C.O.D. *collect on delivery*
2. Col. *Colonel or Colorado*
3. bu. *bushel*
4. bdl. *bundle*
5. B.C. *Before Christ*
6. Aug. *August*
7. ans. *answer*
8. a.m. or A.M. *before noon*
9. alt. *altitude*
10. Ala. *Alabama*

Use at least three of the above abbreviations in sentences. Write them on the lines below. Underline the abbreviations you have used.

Answers vary

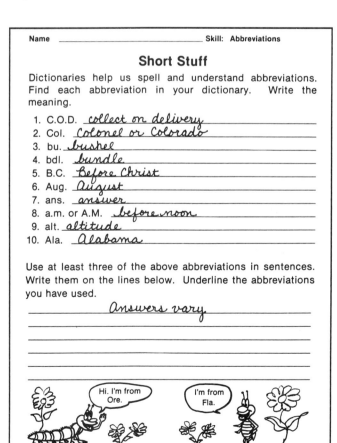

Hi. I'm from Ore.   I'm from Fla.

Page 67

Name _____ Skill: Abbreviations

More Short Stuff

Find these abbreviations in your dictionary. Use each one in a sentence.

1. AEC *Atomic Energy Commission*
2. Adv. *Advertisement*
3. A.D. *since Christ was born*
4. BA or AB *Bachelor of Arts*
5. cu. *cubic*
6. doz. *dozen*
7. D.P. *displaced person*
8. ct. *cent*
9. Dr. *Doctor*
10. D.S.T. *Daylight Savings Time*

Can you find other abbreviations in your dictionary? List two or more and tell what they mean.

Answers vary

Lt. Byrd   P.F.C. Tweetie reporting, sir.

Page 68

Answer Key

Picture Perfect Clues

Name _____ Skill: Illustrations

Sometimes dictionaries contain pictures that help us understand the meanings of words. Find the words below and draw a picture that shows the meaning of each word below.

1. conning tower — tower on a submarine
2. coot — bird
3. cope — long priestly coat
4. cupola — rounded dome on roof
5. decanter — glass bottle with stopper
6. derby — hat
7. dibble — pointed tool
8. dirigible — blimp
9. discus — throwing object
10. curlew — wading bird

Page 69

Scavenger Hunt

Name _____ Skill: Word Meanings

Hunt through your dictionary to find each answer. Check the underlined word.

1. Why can't an animal be a large mite?
   A mite is small.
2. Why can't you fight a Warsaw?
   It is a place.
3. Why can't you curl your hair in rivulets?
   It is a stream.
4. Why don't cows graze in a pastern?
   It is part of a horse's foot.
5. Why can't you get things to stick on paste board?
   It is cardboard.
6. Can you hear something grackle? __ why?
   No, it is a bird.
7. Tell one job a gaucho could do.
   any cowboy type work
8. Why can't you gauge out a hole?
   It is a measuring instrument.
9. Why isn't a carillon a good car?
   It is a set of bells.
10. Why don't we find cars in a carmine?
    It is a color.

I've had quite a problem with mites this year.

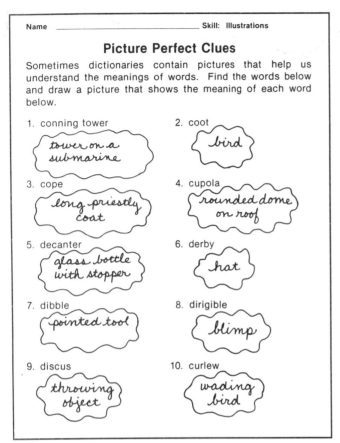

Page 70

Gone Hunting

Name _____ Skill: Meanings

Hunt through the dictionary to find out what you would do with each of these things or people. Write your answer on the line.

EXAMPLE: clarinet — play it

1. bannock — *eat it*
2. incisor — *bite*
3. carter — *have him drive a cart*
4. gondola — *ride on the water*
5. dovecote — *use it for pigeons*
6. ensign — *fly it*
7. flask — *carry liquid in it*
8. goblet — *drink from it*
9. gooseberry — *put it in a pie*
10. haversack — *carry food in it*
11. Indian club — *swing it*

Will anything up there help a bad case of fleas?

Say...he looks yummy

Let's go!

scratch.

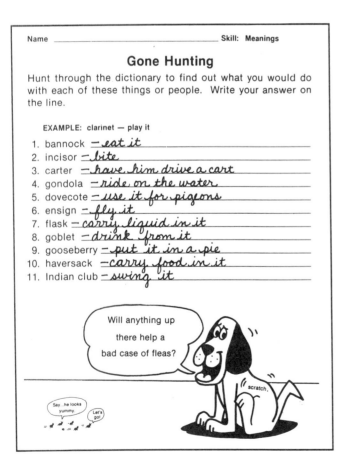

Page 71

Something New

Name _____ Skill: Multiple Meanings

Find the underlined words below in your dictionary. Read each meaning of the word. Now write a sentence using the word with a different meaning than that in the printed sentence. You may use a different form of the word.

EXAMPLE: He was on the last leg of his journey. The table has legs.

1. Did he exercise today?
   Answers vary
2. Did you see the flag flap in the breeze?

3. They saw the Chinese junk.

4. They climbed the flight of stairs.

5. He saw a light flash.

6. He hoped for a good fortune.

7. He committed a foul during the game.

8. They walked through the gallery.

9. They introduced a new food at the show.

10. Did you join the club?

11. Your fingers have joints.

12. The boys were game for anything.

Page 72

Answer Key

Name _____ Skill: Different Words With
the Same Spelling

Answers will vary with dictionary used.

The Same But Different

Two or more words may be spelled the same way.

EXAMPLE: till 1 (til) until
till 2 (til) cultivate; plow
till 3 (til) a small drawer for money

Well, what do you know!

Use your dictionary to find the different words that are spelled like those below. Write one meaning for each different word.

A. batter 1. *beat with repeated blows*
2. *mixture of flour, milk, etc.*
3. *player whose turn it is to bat*

B. baste 1. *drip melted fat on while roasting*
2. *sew with long stitches*

C. bat 1. *a wooden stick*
2. *flying animal*
3. *wink*

D. ash 1. *what remains after burning a thing*
2. *a kind of tree*

E. cue 1. *last word of speech as signal for next speaker*
2. *stick for striking a ball*

F. cricket 1. *an insect*
2. *an English game*
3. *small low stool*

G. junk 1. *rubbish, trash*
2. *a Chinese ship*

Page 73

Name _____ Skill: Special Word Meanings

Special Meanings

Some words have special meanings. By looking for the word dust, we find special meanings such as: bite the dust, lick the dust, or shake the dust off one's feet.

Look for the most important word in each expression below. Find that word in the dictionary. (If it isn't listed, try a different word. The first few were underlined for you.) Write the meaning.

1. catch one's eye *attract one's attention*
2. keep one's head *stay calm*
3. take heart *be encouraged*
4. rack one's brain *think hard*
5. bury the hatchet *make peace*
6. follow in one's footstep *do as another has done*
7. out of sorts *ill, uncomfortable*
8. crocodile tears *false tears*
9. see eye to eye *agree*
10. an eye for an eye *punishment equal to the crime*

Page 74

Name _____ Skill: Accents

What's the Beat?

When we pronounce a word with more than one syllable, we usually accent (say with more force) one of the syllables. An accent mark (′) is placed after that syllable. Try to mark the accented syllable in each word below, then use your dictionary to check your work.

EXAMPLE: Play′ ground

doo dah dah dah dee dee dee!

1. learn′ er
2. flow′ er
3. di vide′
4. dis tinct′
5. cen′ ter
6. cen′ ti pede
7. car′ rot
8. car na′ tion
9. car toon′
10. car′ ton
11. bi′ cy cle
12. ap point′
13. ap′ ple
14. ap pear′
15. a′ ble

thump

tap tap

Page 75

Name _____ Skill: Multiple Meanings

Multiple Meanings

Look at the meanings of each word. Put the number of the meaning used in each sentence below. You may use the same number twice.

good (gud) 1. excellent 2. well-behaved 3. right
4. desirable 5. satisfying 6. pleasant 7. kind, friendly
8. real: genuine 9. benefit

_5_ A. The dinner was good.
_9_ B. What good will it do?
_1_ C. He received a good grade.
_7_ D. Say a good word for me.
_8_ E. It is good money.
_2_ F. He is a good boy.
_4_ G. That is a good book for children to read.
_3_ H. That answer is good.
_6_ I. Have a good time.

Let's see.

dispatch (dis pach) 1. send off for a purpose 2. send a letter etc.
3. A written message 4. get something done promptly 5. finish off

_3_ J. The dispatch arrived.
_2_ K. He dispatched the telegram.
_1_ L. He dispatched a messenger to inform the President.
_4_ M. She did the job with dispatch.
_5_ N. They dispatched the cake.

Page 76

123

Answer Key

What's He Talking About

The dictionary shows pronunciation (the way to say) of each word. Look at the respellings in parenthesis ( ) below. Write the word, spelling it correctly. The pronunciation key at the front of your dictionary will help you.

1. Do you know how to (də vĭd´)? *divide*
2. Did he (kəm plēt´) his work? *complete*
3. She put (ī´ ə dīn) on the cut. *iodine*
4. The (jŭr i) found him guilty. *jury*
5. Mom is at the (mär´ kit) *market*
6. A (pla tō´) is a plain in the mountains. *plateau*
7. Put lots of food on my (plāt). *plate*
8. (Rō) the boat to shore. *Row*
9. They sat on the (san´ di) shore. *sandy*
10. I feel (sik). *sick*
11. Take your (tern). *turn*
12. I (wil) do the job. *will*

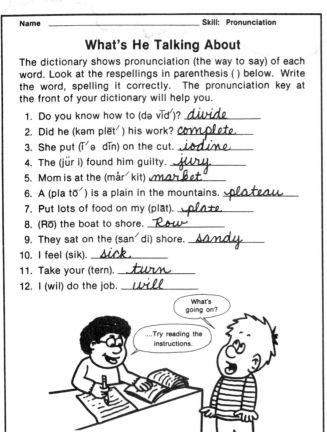

Page 77

Root Words

Answers vary with dictionary used.

To find the meaning of a word, we must look for the root word. Example: To find the meaning of painted, we would look for paint.

Write the root word in each word below. Be sure to put in any letters that were taken out when an ending was added. Look for the root word in the dictionary and write the first meaning.

1. appointed *appoint* 1. *decide on*
2. bigger *big* 1. *large*
3. composing *compose* 1. *make up*
4. dabbling *dabble* 1. *to wet by little dips*
5. discouraged *discourage* 1. *take away courage*
6. divinities *divinity* 1. *divine being*
7. finances *finance* 1. *money matter*
8. gassing *gas* 1. *vapor*
9. generalities *generality* 1. *a general or vague statement*
10. gasped *gasp* 1. *catching breath with mouth open*
11. goodies *goody* 1. *something good to eat*
12. leakiest *leaky* 1. *leaking*

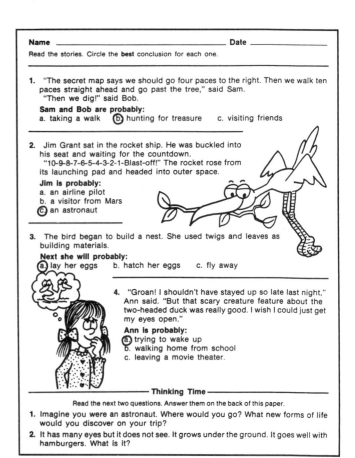

Page 78

Dictionary Merits*

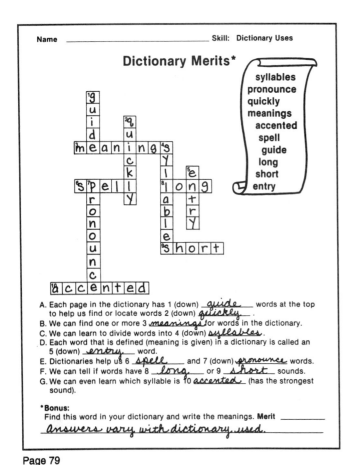

syllables
pronounce
quickly
meanings
accented
spell
guide
long
short
entry

A. Each page in the dictionary has 1 (down) *guide* words at the top to help us find or locate words 2 (down) *quickly*.
B. We can find one or more 3 *meanings* for words in the dictionary.
C. We can learn to divide words into 4 (down) *syllables*.
D. Each word that is defined (meaning is given) in a dictionary is called an 5 (down) *entry* word.
E. Dictionaries help us 6 *spell* and 7 (down) *pronounce* words.
F. We can tell if words have 8 *long* or 9 *short* sounds.
G. We can even learn which syllable is 10 *accented* (has the strongest sound).

*Bonus:
    Find this word in your dictionary and write the meanings. Merit _____
    Answers vary with dictionary used.

Page 79

Read the stories. Circle the **best** conclusion for each one.

1. "The secret map says we should go four paces to the right. Then we walk ten paces straight ahead and go past the tree," said Sam.
   "Then we dig!" said Bob.
   Sam and Bob are probably:
   a. taking a walk   ⓑ hunting for treasure   c. visiting friends

2. Jim Grant sat in the rocket ship. He was buckled into his seat and waiting for the countdown.
   "10-9-8-7-6-5-4-3-2-1-Blast-off!" The rocket rose from its launching pad and headed into outer space.
   Jim is probably:
   a. an airline pilot
   b. a visitor from Mars
   ⓒ an astronaut

3. The bird began to build a nest. She used twigs and leaves as building materials.
   Next she will probably:
   ⓐ lay her eggs   b. hatch her eggs   c. fly away

4. "Groan! I shouldn't have stayed up so late last night," Ann said. "But that scary creature feature about the two-headed duck was really good. I wish I could just get my eyes open."
   Ann is probably:
   ⓐ trying to wake up
   b. walking home from school
   c. leaving a movie theater.

— **Thinking Time** —
Read the next two questions. Answer them on the back of this paper.
1. Imagine you were an astronaut. Where would you go? What new forms of life would you discover on your trip?
2. It has many eyes but it does not see. It grows under the ground. It goes well with hamburgers. What is it?

Page 80

Answer Key

Page 81

Name _____ Date _____

Read the stories. Circle the **best** conclusion for each one.

1. These people use refrigerators to keep their food from freezing. It is so cold where they live that food will freeze if left outside.
   You can guess these people are called:
   a. Chinese   b. Arabs   ⓒ Eskimos

2. Mary found an old mug in the cupboard. "I wonder why Mother put this mug away?" Mary asked. She washed it out. Then she put some tomato juice in it and began drinking. Mary looked at her blouse. "Now I know why we never use it," she said.
   You can guess:
   ⓐ The mug had a crack in it.
   b. The mug was dirty.
   c. The mug had no handle.

3. The paint on the house was peeling. The front window was broken. Weeds grew wild in the yard and the front gate creaked.
   You can guess the house was:
   a. new   b. beautiful   ⓒ deserted

4. Bernie has strange tastes. He loves rattlesnake meat and chocolate-covered ants. His favorite food is a fruit. When Bernie eats it, he says, "Here's to Sour Power!"
   You can guess his favorite food is a:
   a. banana   ⓑ lemon   c. plum

─── Thinking Time ───

Read the next two questions. Answer them on the back of this paper.
1. What happened to Mary's blouse in the second story?
2. Make up a story about the people who lived in the house in the third story.

Page 81

Page 82

Name _____ Date _____

Read the stories. Circle the **best** conclusion for each one.

1. The rain poured down for days. Every day the river rose higher and higher.
   If it did not stop raining soon, there would be:
   a. a hurricane   ⓑ a flood   c. an earthquake

2. Tom told Sara to meet him at his house after school. When Sara reached his house, she knocked on the door. There was no answer so she just walked inside. It was dark in the room. As Sara turned on the lights she heard several people yell, "Surprise!"
   You can guess it was:
   a. a robber
   ⓑ Sara's birthday
   c. the last day of school

3. Fred stood at the top of the snow-covered hill and leaned on his poles.
   He was all set to:
   ⓐ ski   b. skate   c. bobsled

4. Pat put $.75 in his pocket for lunch money. When he got to school he ran into several of his friends. He stopped to talk to them for awhile.
   "Hey! I just found three quarters on the ground!" his friend Jack yelled.
   You can guess:
   a. The money had been lying there for several days.
   b. The money belonged to the school nurse.
   ⓒ Pat's pocket had a hole in it.

─── Thinking Time ───

Read the next two questions. Answer them on the back of this paper.
1. What might happen to a dam during a flood? Describe what would happen to the houses in the area.
2. What is wrong with this story? Marsha took off her skates and put on her shoes. Then she went skating.

Page 82

Page 83

Name _____ Date _____

Read the stories. Circle the **best** conclusion for each one.

1. Matt was in the kitchen making dinner. Sally was in the living room watching the evening news on TV.
   It is probably:
   a. 7:30 a.m.   b. 12:00 m.   ⓒ 6:00 p.m.

2. Andy found a basketball in an empty lot. "This is great! All it needs is some air," he said. He pumped it up and began bouncing it. "Hey, this ball is no good," Andy said.
   You can guess the ball:
   a. was the wrong color
   ⓑ had a hole in it
   c. was too small

3. Polly went for a swim in the ocean. Suddenly she noticed a large fin sticking out of the water. It began circling her.
   You can guess the fin belonged to a:
   a. whale   b. swordfish   ⓒ shark

4. As Paul watched the movie, his eyes grew bigger and bigger. He gulped several times. His hands shook and were icy cold. During certain parts, he put his hands over his eyes.
   You can guess the movie was:
   a. funny
   ⓑ scary
   c. sad

─── Thinking Time ───

Read the next two questions. Answer them on the back of this paper.
1. In the second story, what do you think Andy did with the ball?
2. What do you think Polly did in the third story?

Page 83

Page 84

Name _____ Date _____

Read the stories. Circle the **best** conclusion for each one.

1. It is spring. The orange tree in our backyard is covered with white blossoms.
   You can guess that the tree will soon:
   a. lose its leaves   b. have red blossoms   ⓒ bear fruit

2. Mordor was a visitor from Mars. He had four ears and three arms. One day Peggy walked up behind him. "Hello, Peggy," Mordor said without turning around. "How did you know it was me?" Peggy asked.
   You can guess that Mordor:
   a. had eyes in the back of his head
   was Peggy's father
   ⓒ could only see things in front of him

3. Brian entered the bubblegum-blowing contest. He blew a huge bubble. It got bigger and bigger. He continued blowing. It got even bigger.
   You can guess that the bubble:
   a. grew bigger than Brian   b. floated away   ⓒ burst

4. Becky's house was overrun by mice. She set mousetraps all through the house. In each trap she put a small chunk of cheese. The next day she checked the traps.
   "These mice are too smart for me," she said.
   The mice probably:
   ⓐ ate the cheese and ran away
   b. moved away
   c. didn't like cheese

─── Thinking Time ───

Read the next two questions. Answer them on the back of this paper.
1. Draw a picture of Mordor.
2. Make up a conversation between two mice. Imagine they live at Becky's house.

Page 84

Page 85

Name _____ Date _____

Read the stories. Circle the **best** conclusion for each one.

1. Tom looked out the window. "It looks like a great day for kite flying," he said.
   You can guess it is probably:
   a. sunny   ⓑ windy   c. cloudy

2. Jack was late for school. He dressed quickly and dashed out the door. When he got to school he sat down at his desk. He glanced down at his feet and his face turned bright red.
   You can guess:
   a. He had worn his best pair of socks.
   b. His socks were too big.
   ⓒ Each sock was a different color.

3. First, Mike polished his shoes until they shone. Then, he shaved and patted his face with after-shave lotion. Finally, he put on his new black suit.
   Mike is probably going to:
   ⓐ a dance   b. the movies   c. a baseball game

4. Jane was going to take a bath. She turned on the faucets and began running the bath water. "Jane, can you help me a minute?" her mother asked. Jane helped her mother set the table for dinner. Then she looked up at the ceiling. She quickly ran upstairs.
   You can guess:
   a. The ceiling had a hole in it.
   ⓑ The bath tub was overflowing.
   c. The ceiling light had gone out.

─── Thinking Time ───

Read the next two questions. Answer them on the back of this paper.
1. How old do you think Mike is in the third story? Why?
2. What will happen next in the fourth story?

Page 85

Page 86

Name _____ Date _____

Read the stories. Circle the **best** conclusion for each one.

1. He is old, but stands tall. He has a white beard and wears a red, white and blue outfit. He is a symbol of America to people all over the world.
   You can guess he is:
   a. George Washington   ⓑ Uncle Sam   c. Abraham Lincoln

2. Debbie had just bought a new sports car. She decided to go for a drive. Debbie turned on the motor and put her foot on the gas. After driving just a short way, she heard a siren behind her.
   You can guess that Debbie:
   ⓐ was driving too fast
   b. had run out of gas
   c. didn't have her seat belt on

3. The rain has ended. Now the sun is coming out. The raindrops are sparkling in the sunlight.
   If we are lucky we may see:
   ⓐ a rainbow   b. a pot of gold   c. stars

4. Dad checked everything in the car. "We have sleeping bags, a lantern, a tent, firewood and food. Looks like we're ready to go."
   He looked once more and then he smiled. "There's only one problem. There's no room for us!"
   The family in this story is probably:
   a. going sailing
   b. going on a picnic
   ⓒ going camping

─── Thinking Time ───

Read the next two questions. Answer them on the back of this paper.
1. Imagine you are going on a picnic. What are some things you will need to take along?
2. In the second story, Debbie hears a siren. Who is following her? What will happen to her?

Page 86

Answer Key

Page 89

Name _____ Date _____

Read the stories. Circle the **best** conclusion for each one.

1. It looks like a flying eggbeater. It can move up, down, sideways or hover in the air. "Is it a bird?"
You **can guess** it is:
a. a jet   b. an airplane   **c. a helicopter** (circled)

2. It was a wet, cold morning. Paul put on his bearskin and reached for his club. He crawled out of his cave. He could see a huge dinosaur in the distance. "Paul, it's time to get up. You'll be late for school," his mother said.
Paul was probably:
a. dreaming
b. a real caveman (circled)
c. lost

3. The sap from this tree is used to make many different things. Some of the things are tires, balls and rain boots.
You can guess this tree is called a:
a. metal tree   **b. rubber tree** (circled)   c. leather tree

4. Bob decided today was a good day to try his experiment. He took an egg from the refrigerator and went outside. Then he cracked the egg over the sidewalk. It began to try as if it were in a pan on the stove.
It was probably a _____ day.
a. warm
b. very hot (circled)
c. cold

Thinking Time
Read the next two questions. Answer them on the back of the paper.
1. Trees have many valuable uses. Name three.
2. What's wrong with this story? Sally had to clean the house. She washed all the dishes. Then she unmade all the beds. Finally, she swept the floors.

Page 92

Name _____ Date _____

Read the stories. Circle the **best** conclusion for each one.

1. He travels all over the country. Sometimes he carries loads of fruits and vegetables to market. Other times he carries lumber or gasoline.
You can guess he is a:
a. policeman   **b. truck driver** (circled)   c. farmer

2. Jack and Jean wanted to go to the zoo. When they got into Jack's car, he looked at the dashboard. "Uh-oh," Jack said. "I think we'll have to walk to the park instead."
You can guess:
a. Jack had forgotten his keys.
b. The car was out of gas. (circled)
c. The zoo was closed.

3. Roger and John built a sand castle at the beach. It had four towers, a drawbridge and a moat. After they left, the tide came in.
When they returned the next day, the castle:
a. was gone (circled)   b. was floating in the ocean   c. was still there

4. Gale and her family went on a camping trip. There was a sign posted at the campgrounds. It said: Watch Out For Bears. The family unpacked their things and went for a walk. When they returned, they discovered all their food was gone. Their tent was ripped apart, too.
You can guess:
a. There had been a big thunderstorm.
b. Squirrels had wandered through the camp.
c. Bears had visited the camp. (circled)

Thinking Time
Read the next two questions. Answer them on the back of this paper.
1. What should the family in the fourth story have done to protect their food and tent?
2. If you had one wish, what would you wish for?

Page 88

Name _____ Date _____

Read the stories. Circle the **best** conclusion for each one.

1. Ben looked at the calendar on his bedroom wall. The date June 16th was circled in red. "Only one more week until the last day!" he said happily.
You can guess June 16th is:
a. the last day of school   **b. the last day of vacation** (circled)   c. Ben's birthday

2. Becky had studied very hard for the history test. Mrs. Brown, her teacher, passed out the tests to the students. "Remember," she said, "the test is on Chapters 6-9." "Oh, no!" Becky cried.
You can guess Becky:
a. studied the wrong chapters (circled)
b. thinks she will do well on the test
c. is in the wrong room

3. Barbara took a step forward and began sinking slowly. "Help! I'm stuck!" she cried.
Barbara had probably:
a. fallen into a hole   **b. gotten caught in quicksand** (circled)   c. fallen into a stream

4. George bought two pieces of candy. He popped both pieces into his mouth and began chewing harder. He chewed harder. Now the candy stuck to his teeth. He chewed harder. Now the candy stuck to his tongue. "Hi, George. How are you?" Rob asked. "Mmmhmmm" George said.
George was probably eating:
a. taffy (circled)
b. chocolate bars
c. sour balls

Thinking Time
Read the next two questions. Answer them on the back of this paper.
1. Name three kinds of candy that take a long time to eat.
2. Imagine you are taking a trip through a jungle. What are some things you will have to watch out for?

Page 91

Name _____ Date _____

Read the stories. Circle the **best** conclusion for each one.

1. "What a day! First I get a sore throat so I can't roar. Then an elephant steps on my paw. I don't feel much like the King of the Jungle today!"
You can guess I am a:
a. tiger   **b. lion** (circled)   c. bear

2. Jeff was practicing a new trick. First he put a tablecloth on the table. Next he set the table with plates and cups. Then he tried to whisk the cloth off the table without disturbing the cups or plates.
Jeff probably:
a. breaks a lot of cups and plates
b. gets the trick right the first time (circled)
c. has a very happy mother

3. Mark and Sue visited a strange planet. There were ten-foot carrot trees. Enormous spinach leaves were used to make roofs. Potatoes were as large as Earth's pumpkins.
You can guess this planet was called:
a. Fruitworld   b. Spinachoid   **c. Vegetableania** (circled)

4. "On your mark, get set, go!" Sally, Lucy and Dana began running at top speed. When they crossed the finish line they were all panting. Their running times were: Dana at 2 minutes, Lucy at 1 minute 30 seconds and Sally at 1 minute 32 seconds.
You can tell _____ **won the race.**
a. Dana
b. Lucy (circled)
c. Sally

Thinking Time
Read the next two questions. Answer them on the back of this paper.
1. What is your favorite trick? How long did it take you to learn it?
2. What's wrong with this story? Pam just turned twelve. This morning she dressed and ate breakfast. Then she drove her car to school.

Page 87

Name _____ Date _____

Read the stories. Circle the **best** conclusion for each one.

1. Amanda was reading an exciting story. It was about a woman who had magic powers. She could fly and turn carrots into gold.
Amanda was probably reading a:
a. fairy tale (circled)   b. true story   c. history book

2. Peggy piled meat, lettuce, cheese and tomatoes on top of some bread. "This needs some mayonnaise," she said. She found a jar marked mayonnaise in the refrigerator. "Yuck, this tastes awful!" she said. Just then Roger started looking in the refrigerator. "Hey, have you seen my jar of paste?" he asked.
You can guess that:
a. The mayonnaise jar had paste in it. (circled)
b. The mayonnaise was spoiled.
c. Peggy put too much salt on the sandwich.

3. Nat looked out the window. He saw a jet take off. Then he saw a small plane land on the airfield. Meanwhile, another plane moved down the runway.
Nat is probably at the:
a. airport (circled)   b. space center   c. bus station

4. "The trees are so thick, I can hardly see!" Bob said. "I think that hanging vine is really a snake!" Pam screamed. "Shh! I hear a lion growling!" Sam whispered.
They are probably:
a. in the mountains
b. in the jungle (circled)
c. near the ocean

Thinking Time
Read the next two questions. Answer them on the back of this paper.
1. What should Peggy have done in the second story?
2. In the third story what do you think Nat is about to do?

Page 90

Name _____ Date _____

Read the stories. Circle the **best** conclusion for each one.

1. "Gee, I wish I were like Jeff," said Nan. "He really has a green thumb. All his plants do well. I guess I have a brown thumb."
Nan is probably:
a. good at   **b. not good at**   gardening. (circled b)
c. not interested in

2. Elaine wanted to get the spy ring that unlocked secret messages. For two weeks she ate Zowie cereal every day.
You can guess Elaine:
a. loved Zowie cereal
b. had to mail in cereal boxtops to get the ring (circled)
c. only had cereal in the house

3. Tim was thinking about a round, flat pie. It was covered with tomato sauce, cheese and sausage. Tim went to the phone and started dialing a number.
You can guess he:
a. ordered a pizza (circled)   b. called a friend   c. made his own pizza

4. Rachel sat in the machine and turned the dial. The machine began shaking and bright lights were flashing. When the shaking ended, she got out. She saw a castle at the top of a hill. A man dressed in armor rode out of the castle on a white horse.
You can guess Rachel had traveled:
a. into the past (circled)
b. into the future
c. to modern-day England

Thinking Time
Read the next two questions. Answer them on the back of this paper.
1. Can you make a special kind of food? Describe how you prepare it step-by-step.
2. Paul bought some hay and oats at the feed store. What kind of animal do you think Paul owns?

Answer Key

Page 93

Name ___ **Date** ___

Read the stories. Circle the best conclusion for each one.

1. This cartoon hero loves carrots. He also loves to play jokes on people. His favorite saying is, "What's up, Doc?"
   You can guess he is:
   a. Mickey Mouse b. Daffy Duck **c. Bugs Bunny** *(circled)*

2. All of Susie's toys were packed into a big box. Her suitcase was filled with clothes. Her mother had just finished putting all the dishes and pans into crates. Just then a big truck pulled up in the driveway.
   You can guess Susie and her family are:
   a. getting ready for a trip
   b. moving to a new city *(circled)*
   c. having a garage sale

3. My dog Lad is very friendly. However, he doesn't realize how big and strong he is. He is even bigger than I am. When I come home from school, Lad dashes straight towards me.
   You can guess he:
   a. knocks me down *(circled)* b. sits quietly c. jumps over me

4. My friend Jake works at the circus. Sometimes he shows off at home. When he washes the dishes he balances a teacup on his nose. Then he tosses the dishes from one hand to another. When Jake washes dishes, his mother always closes her eyes.
   You can guess Jake is a:
   a. lion tamer
   b. tightrope walker
   c. juggler *(circled)*

—— Thinking Time ——
1. Who is your favorite cartoon hero? Why?
2. How old do you think Lad's owner might be? Why?

Page 94

Name ___ **Date** ___

Read the stories. Circle the best conclusion for each one.

1. They are very hard workers. They can carry objects several times larger than they are. One of them can even carry a huge breadcrumb all by himself!
   They are probably:
   a. horses b. people **c. ants** *(circled)*

2. Thump! Dad and Mom were awakened in the middle of the night. Someone was in the house! Dad took a flashlight and crept downstairs. As he walked through the kitchen, the cat dashed out the door.
   The noise was probably caused by:
   a. a robber
   b. the cat *(circled)*
   c. a dog

3. Wherever Nancy walked, she could see the ocean. There was nothing to eat but coconuts. Nancy's clothes were torn. Worst of all, her boat had sunk. Now she could never leave!
   Nancy is probably:
   a. on a ship **b. on an island** *(circled)* c. lost in the woods

4. My dog Rover can do a lot of tricks. When I call him, he rolls over. When I tell him to roll over, he goes to sleep. His best trick of all is standing still.
   This year at the dog show, Rover will probably:
   a. win many prizes
   b. not win any prizes *(circled)*
   c. do several new tricks

—— Thinking Time ——
1. In the second story the word "thump" tells us something happened. What do you think it was?
2. Nancy has a problem in the third story. What would you do if you were her?

Page 95

Name ___ **Date** ___

Read the stories. Circle the best conclusion for each one.

1. Carl found some nails in a field. He could tell they had been there for quite awhile.
   The nails were probably:
   a. shiny b. black **c. rusty** *(circled)*

2. Ray waxed and polished his car. Next he watered the lawn. Finally, he washed all the windows on his house from the outside. Just then dark clouds began to gather in the sky. "I should have known this would happen!" he groaned.
   You can guess:
   a. It will rain. *(circled)*
   b. There will be an earthquake.
   c. It will snow.

3. Willie loves candy, gum, ice cream and cake. He eats loads of sweets every day.
   You can guess Willie:
   a. doesn't have good teeth *(circled)* b. is very strong c. is very tall

4. Connie sawed some boards in two. Then she hammered the boards into the wooden frame. Soon she would be ready to put up the roof.
   You can guess Connie is building a:
   a. bed
   b. house *(circled)*
   c. ten-story building

—— Thinking Time ——
1. In the third story, Willie eats a lot of sweets. Name foods that Willie should eat to be healthy.
2. Why was Ray unhappy about the change in the weather?

Page 96

Weather or Not — **Name** ___

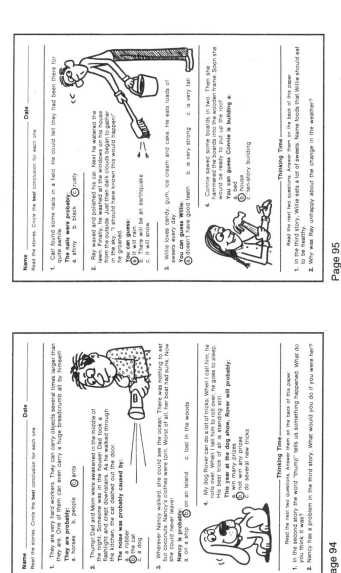

1. The main idea of this story is:
   a. changing weather *(circled)*
   b. a cloudy day
   c. an old umbrella

2. Anita liked:
   a. the sun *(circled)*
   b. the moon
   c. TV

3. Anita said she wanted to:
   a. be ready for the rain
   b. be ready for snow
   c. be ready for any kind of weather *(circled)*

4. Drenched means:
   a. very warm
   b. very cold
   c. very wet *(circled)*

5. You can tell that:
   a. The weatherman was right.
   b. The weatherman was wrong. *(circled)*
   c. The TV was broken.

6. The first thing Anita wore was:
   a. a raincoat and boots
   b. snowshoes and a jacket
   c. a sundress and sunglasses *(circled)*

*On the back of this paper, write about your favorite kind of weather and why you like it.

Page 97

The Scary Movie — **Name** ___

1. The main idea of this story is:
   a. eating popcorn
   b. screaming in a movie
   c. seeing a scary movie *(circled)*

2. How did Hilda like the movie?
   a. She didn't like it.
   b. She thought it was funny.
   c. She liked it a lot. *(circled)*

3. The movie was called:
   a. The Vampire Meets Godzilla *(circled)*
   b. The Vampire and the Bears
   c. Frankenstein and his Friends

4. Risk means:
   a. taking a bath
   b. taking a chance *(circled)*
   c. seeing a movie

5. You can tell that:
   a. No one was scared.
   b. Only Hilda was scared.
   c. Many people were scared. *(circled)*

6. Before seeing the movie, Hilda:
   a. ate her lunch
   b. read the newspaper
   c. called a friend *(circled)*

*On the back of this paper, write a paragraph about the kind of movie you like best. Why do you like it?

Page 98

Seeing is Believing — **Name** ___

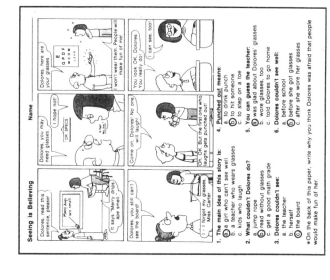

1. The main idea of this story is:
   a. a girl who can't see well *(circled)*
   b. a teacher who wears glasses
   c. kids who laugh

2. What couldn't Dolores do?
   a. jump rope
   b. read without glasses *(circled)*
   c. get a good math grade

3. Dolores couldn't see:
   a. the teacher
   b. herself
   c. the board *(circled)*

4. Punched out means:
   a. to drink punch
   b. to hit someone *(circled)*
   c. to step on a toe

5. You can guess the teacher:
   a. was glad about Dolores' glasses *(circled)*
   b. wore glasses, too
   c. told Dolores to go home

6. Dolores couldn't see well:
   a. before school
   b. before she got glasses *(circled)*
   c. after she wore her glasses

*On the back of this paper, write why you think Dolores was afraid that people would make fun of her.

Answer Key

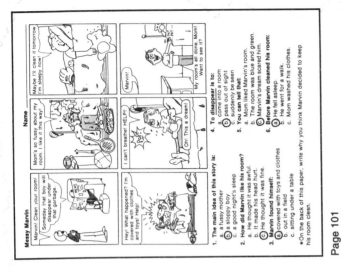

Messy Marvin

1. The main idea of this story is:
   - a. a fussy mother (circled)
   - b. a sloppy boy
   - c. a good night's sleep
2. How did Marvin like his room?
   - a. He thought it was awful.
   - b. It made his head hurt.
   - c. He thought it was fine. (circled)
3. Marvin found himself:
   - a. covered with toys and clothes (circled)
   - b. out in a field
   - c. sitting under a table
4. To disappear is to:
   - a. come into a room
   - b. pass out of sight (circled)
   - c. suddenly be seen
5. You can tell that:
   - a. Mom liked Marvin's room.
   - b. The room was blue and green.
   - c. Marvin's dream scared him. (circled)
6. Before Marvin cleaned his room:
   - a. He fell asleep. (circled)
   - b. He went for a walk.
   - c. He washed his clothes.

*On the back of this paper, write why you think Marvin decided to keep his room clean.

Page 101

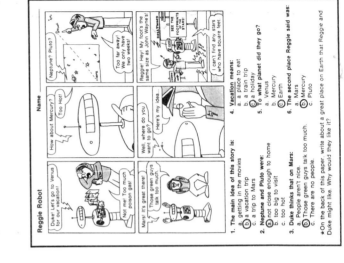

Reggie Robot

1. The main idea of this story is:
   - a. getting in the movies (circled)
   - b. a vacation trip
   - c. a trip to Mars
2. Neptune and Pluto were:
   - a. not close enough to home (circled)
   - b. too big to visit
   - c. too hot
3. Duke thinks that on Mars:
   - a. People aren't nice.
   - b. Those green guys talk too much. (circled)
   - c. There are no people.
4. Vacation means:
   - a. a place to eat
   - b. a train trip
   - c. a holiday (circled)
5. To what planet did they go?
   - a. Venus
   - b. Mercury
   - c. Earth (circled)
6. The second place Reggie said was:
   - a. Mars
   - b. Mercury (circled)
   - c. Pluto

*On the back of this paper, write about a great place on Earth that Reggie and Duke might like. Why would they like it?

Page 104

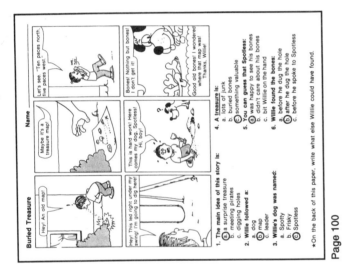

Buried Treasure

1. The main idea of this story is:
   - a. a surprise treasure (circled)
   - b. meeting pirates
   - c. digging holes
2. Willie followed a:
   - a. dog
   - b. map (circled)
   - c. leader
3. Willie's dog was named:
   - a. Spotty
   - b. Frisky
   - c. Spotless (circled)
4. A treasure is:
   - a. lots of junk
   - b. buried bones
   - c. something valuable (circled)
5. You can guess that Spotless:
   - a. was happy to see his bones
   - b. didn't care about his bones (circled)
   - c. bit Willie on the hand
6. Willie found the bones:
   - a. before he dug the hole
   - b. after he dug the hole (circled)
   - c. before he spoke to Spotless

*On the back of this paper, write what else Willie could have found.

Page 100

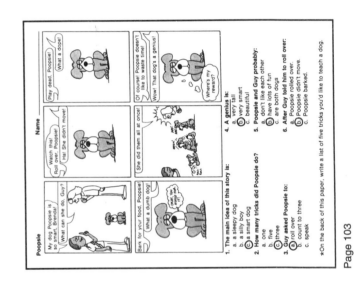

Poopsie

1. The main idea of this story is:
   - a. a sleepy dog
   - b. a silly boy
   - c. a smart dog (circled)
2. How many tricks did Poopsie do?
   - a. one
   - b. five
   - c. three (circled)
3. Guy asked Poopsie to:
   - a. roll over
   - b. count to three
   - c. speak (circled)
4. A genius is:
   - a. very tall
   - b. very smart (circled)
   - c. beautiful
5. Poopsie and Guy probably:
   - a. don't like each other
   - b. have lots of fun (circled)
   - c. are both dogs
6. After Guy told him to roll over:
   - a. Poopsie rolled over.
   - b. Poopsie didn't move. (circled)
   - c. Poopsie barked.

*On the back of this paper, write a list of five tricks you'd like to teach a dog.

Page 103

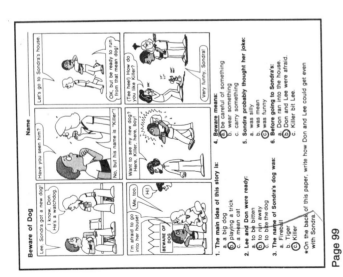

Beware of Dog

1. The main idea of this story is:
   - a. a big dog (circled)
   - b. playing a trick
   - c. a mean cat
2. Lee and Don were ready:
   - a. to run away (circled)
   - b. to be bitten
   - c. to bite the dog
3. The name of Sondra's dog was:
   - a. Fireball
   - b. Tiger
   - c. Killer (circled)
4. Beware means:
   - a. be careful of something (circled)
   - b. wear something
   - c. carry something
5. Sondra probably thought her joke:
   - a. was silly
   - b. was mean
   - c. was funny (circled)
6. Before going to Sondra's:
   - a. Don ran into the house.
   - b. Don and Lee were afraid. (circled)
   - c. Killer bit Lee.

*On the back of this paper, write how Don and Lee could get even with Sondra.

Page 99

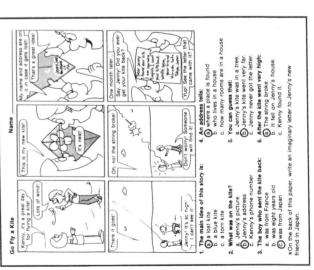

Go Fly a Kite

1. The main idea of this story is:
   - a. a lost kite (circled)
   - b. a blue kite
   - c. a torn kite
2. What was on the kite?
   - a. Jenny's picture
   - b. Jenny's address (circled)
   - c. Kenny's phone number
3. The boy who sent the kite back:
   - a. was from France
   - b. was eight years old
   - c. was from Japan (circled)
4. An address tells:
   - a. where a place is found (circled)
   - b. who lives in a house
   - c. how many rooms are in a house
5. You can guess that:
   - a. Jenny's kite was in a tree.
   - b. Jenny's kite went very far. (circled)
   - c. Jenny never got the letter.
6. After the kite went very high:
   - a. The string broke. (circled)
   - b. It fell on Jenny's house.
   - c. Kenny found it.

*On the back of this paper, write an imaginary letter to Jenny's new friend in Japan.

Page 102